MySpace TO
SACRED SPACE

Also by Christian Piatt
Lost: A Search for Meaning

Complete results of the Piatts' survey on young adult
spirituality are available at www.christianpiatt.com.

MySpace TO
SACRED SPACE

God for a New Generation

Christian Piatt
Amy Piatt

CHALICE
PRESS
ST. LOUIS, MISSOURI

Cover art: Big Cheese Photo, L.L.C.
Cover and interior design: Elizabeth Wright

Visit Chalice Press on the World Wide Web at
www.chalicepress.com

10 9 8 7 6 5 4 3 2 1   07 08 09 10 11 12

Library of Congress Cataloging–in–Publication Data

(pending)

Printed in the United States of America

Contents

Acknowledgments   vii

Introduction   1

I Love to Tell the Story   11

Low Expectations

Retreat

Loss of Absolutes

A Sense of Mystery

Amy's Story

An Overarching Purpose

The God Image   33

A Generation Adrift

Weak Ties, High Mobility

Relationship over Religion

What We Found

America's Four Gods

Now What?

The Coffeehouse Myth   53

The Starbucks Session

Jesus and Java

Habit, Tradition, and Ritual   67

Habit

Tradition

Ritual

A Crisis of Imagination

Story, Experience, and Ritual

Rites of Passage

Sex and Money

Addiction   91

    College, Catharsis, Crisis (As Told by Christian)

    The Human Condition

    Doing What We Hate

    Steps to Recovery

    An Addiction Epidemic

    Our Family Intervention (As Told by Amy)

    Jake's Story

    Numbers Don't Lie

God of Rock   109

    Fair to Compare?

    Christian's Story

    A Window to the Divine

Who May Serve?   129

    Seminary Trends

    The Great Divide

    Drawing Lines, Crossing Lines

    Eric's Story

    Staying at the Table

Church of the Prodigal Child   141

    Who Are They?

    Brenda and Sam's Story

    Jake on the Church

    Spiritual but Not Religious

Conclusion   159

Notes   163

Acknowledgments

From Amy Piatt

Mom and Dad, I thank you for giving me life, love, and encouragement.

Christian, thanks for being patient with me on this project.

To Mattias, thank you for teaching me more about God every day.

I love you all.

From Christian Piatt

To those who shared of their time, stories, and hearts to make this project possible, I offer my respect.

To my mother, Linda, who first taught me what it means to be a person of faith, I offer my gratitude.

To my son, Mattias, who exhibits both an insatiable curiosity and a passionate love for life, I offer my hope.

Introduction

August 2006 was a landmark month for MySpace, the international Web-based interactive networking service. First, it became the most visited site in the world, overcoming former title holders Yahoo! and Google. A little more than a week later, it exceeded 100 million members, equivalent to one third of the entire population of the United States. In January of 2005, the site boasted 10 million member pages; eleven months later, that number quadrupled. By the end of December 2006, MySpace topped 143 million new member pages, at a pace of approximately 2 million a week.

A December 2005 article in *Business Week* describes the generation growing up in a world hardwired with mobile phones, text messaging, blogs, and podcasts as "Generation @." For these young adults and youth, their very social identities are created, promulgated, and reinvented in a virtual landscape. As the article states, "Here you can get a fast pass to the hip music scene, which carries a hefty amount of social currency offline. It's where you go when you need a friend to nurse you through a breakup, a mentor to tutor you on your calculus homework, an address for the party everyone is going to."[1]

MySpace and services like it not only help connect people worldwide: the virtual environment is a critical agent in the formation of one's public identity. The use of avatars, or animated alter egos, is an increasingly popular way for young people to present themselves online, rather than actual photos of themselves. An entire language used in text messaging and instant messaging represents the colloquial shorthand of the online culture. Communication is more likely to be understood by another young person in Thailand than by the parents of the young person who uses such cyberspeak in America. For some online regulars, the archaic machinations of e-mail are already too slow and outmoded to be relevant for much more than business. Limitations such as space and time are rendered inconsequential, yielding to increasingly immediate avenues for sharing information.

MySpace's explosive popularity indicates both a voracious desire for community and a paradigmatic shift in the way people communicate and interrelate. Those who use new technology to meet and communicate with friends see such modern conventions as essential. For those born before the onset of the digital revolution, the constant shifts are sometimes exciting and, at other times, sobering. For those who were born a little bit later, MySpace not only represents the world as it is but as it always has been. To imagine life without such conveniences would be as foreign to them as it would be for the rest of America to imagine a world without power or running water.

Amy and I both have phones that manage half a dozen e-mail accounts, instant message, surf the Web, and more. I run my business from the attic of our house, all based around the Internet. Three years ago, we added a digital video recorder, or DVR–which is like a VCR on steroids–to our media center. Now we can't imagine television viewing without it.

We were explaining to a group of college students about our relatively recent introduction to personal computing around the beginning of college, and one young woman's eyes widened. "How did you write papers? How did you do your research?" She asked in bewilderment.

Woe to you, carbon paper, typewriter manufacturers, and Mr. Dewey Decimal. Your obsolescence has crept in like a thief in the night.

Our three-year-old son, Mattias, gets frustrated when he cannot watch whatever he wants on demand. We strictly limit his television time, but when he does watch, he expects instant access. He calls out his favorite show, sometimes a specific episode, and we pull it up on the DVR. He laps it up like virtual manna. One of his favorite games is to sit on our laps and call out random words while we punch them into Google, the most ubiquitous search engine on the Internet. Within a fraction of a second, we can summon scores of images of anything from Cookie Monster to a full moon.

In his book *Next: The Future Just Happened,* social theorist Michael Lewis notes that tools such as DVRs and Google are turning upside down network television, as well as advertising and the media industry as a whole. Whereas people across the nation used to sit down at the same time to watch the same show, there is no need for that any more. The ability of the viewer to click past commercials renders shotgun marketing strategies of the past practically impotent. Prime time is dead. Guerilla marketing is the lifeblood of any vital company.

Collective experience as a social value has ceded power to personal choice and consumer empowerment.[2] It's a mutiny of unparalleled proportion. As Lewis suggests, it has turned average American consumers into children, who expect to get whatever they want, whenever they want it.

Enter the antiquated behemoth that is the modern church. Built on principles at least a century old, many congregations, and even denominations, are fighting to remain relevant. They may get a member of the youth group to post a Web site or even put podcasts of the minister's message online, but in essence they are the same. The collective fear is that if the church doesn't adapt to the digital shift, it will be left behind forever. But does the church even belong in the digital world and vice versa?

In the postmodern sense, the term *sacred* suggests connection to God, community, and intentionally recognized time and space. In the past, something sacred was exalted or otherworldly: It was set apart. Today, with a growing cynicism about institutional constructs, the sacred is still embraced as significant and holy, but without necessarily being identified as part of the church.

The term *sacred* has origins in the Latin word, *sacer,* meaning "untouchable." It has come to mean that which we seek in wonder and awe. Sacred experiences provide a "set-apart" time and space in which people are inspired and enlivened by a glimpse at what could be: the promise of hope and a vision of God's love realized. Even if only as a mirror, dimly, worship turns us toward God, with the faith that one day we will come to see God "face-to-face,"[3] to touch the untouchable.

In a world where a swelling tide of information and invasive marketing compete for our limited attention, sacred space provides a respite from the appeals to outward satisfaction by engaging our souls rather than our impulses and wallets. But where does the sacred experience find purchase in a culture inured to its own constant white noise? When can sacred moments happen, and how are they evoked? Must they be carefully orchestrated, or can they happen when we least expect them?

Young adults see more marketing messages today in a matter of months than any other generation encountered in an entire lifetime. Businesses spend more than half a trillion dollars every year to grab their attention and purchasing power. As their senses are dulled by the information onslaught, the messages become even more personalized and sophisticated, creeping into the periphery, sometimes at an unconscious level. The consequence of the growing murmur of constant data is a numbing of the senses, and at the same time, an ironic dependence on the steady inflow. We become complicit receptacles for the information the world shoves in our direction, faster than we can digest it.

When we experience the sacred, we awaken the human senses that remind us we are alive. We enter the sacred space, longing to be moved–called–not by high production values and technological gimmickry, but by the beauty and grace of the God of all creation. As we avail ourselves of sanctified moments, we enter them longing for *sanctuary*: asylum from the demands and cacophony of the world, space providing shelter from the persistent impingement of daily life.

We all need a safe place to question, doubt, wonder, and explore. Although we believe that what we seek are answers, what we truly long for is hope and peace. Sacred space grounds us in the present and gives us the chance to envision life on God's terms, creating in that moment a future vision founded in hope. This space invites us to touch, taste, hear, and kneel before a God that transcends time and all other boundaries.

Establishing sacred space outside of familiar church settings and traditions is a challenge for those of us who are a part of the established church. However, as church leaders, we must consider how, when, where, and with whom sacred moments can take place when envisioning the future mission of our collective church. The sacred can be either spontaneous or developed over time, repetitious or out of the ordinary. No set formula exists for creating sacred space. While people used to come to church in order to experience the sacred, now any space, including a coffee shop or living room, can be transformed into holy ground.

As Christians, our call is to light a candle in the darkness. The idea is not new. It is not a fad or trend in worship that statistics show will cram the pews. It is the age-old invitation to follow Jesus. Instead of expecting people to come to church in response to a long-standing invitation, we must go to them. Whether we meet in the corner café or the basement of a bowling alley, when we gather in Jesus' name, that space and time are sacred.

The idea that church happens only when all the vestments are hung and the choir is in place is foreign—or at least uncomfortable—to people who don't attend church. What they want is to connect authentically with others and with God. Their expression and understanding of faith may not be formal or liturgical, but they are valid. This connection is where a journey of faith begins. All the "churchy stuff" can come later and ultimately is secondary. There is a time to learn of Advent. There is a place for the journey of Lent's forty days, but this can only happen if first we Christians go to the people, tell them our story, and take the time to listen to theirs. In doing so, we make room for the spontaneous sacred.

This does not mean the physical church, its rituals, and history have no place in today's world. On the contrary, we still need the set-apart place and time that invites us to come together for a common purpose: to worship God. Whereas the church may have been the point of origin for one's faith journey in the past, now it often becomes a destination. Now people work their way toward community, rather than emerging from it. They develop the longing for experiences of the sacred in whatever context they can. As they recognize that the church is a safe place to further explore their faith, the invitation must remain open.

Scores of books explore the radical changes taking place in modern society. Even in our attempts to help identify some common characteristics of "young adults" as a group, we should note that this group is more disparate in character and more difficult to define categorically than perhaps any other. With the rapid acceleration of technology, information access, and life in general, the stratification of people born within any discrete time period grows ever broader. Today's twenty-year-old generally has less in common with someone twice his or her age than ever before. Further, people resist traditional definitions and labels, creating a fuzzier notion of what exactly we're talking about with regard to young adults.

For our purposes, we consider anyone from the ages of eighteen to forty to be a young adult. One reason we have selected such a wide age range is to ensure that we both are still well within the young-adult spectrum, which makes us feel better. Also, several life-changing experiences occur within this time, during which many people tend to depart from church, beginning with leaving home for the first time to go to college or work. Finally, generally during this time people begin to grow their own families, reinventing the family tree as a part of the ever-expanding continuum. Young adults' focus shifts from themselves to the wants and needs of others; they begin to think more of the future, question their own mortality, and create familial, professional, and social identities with which they may be identified for decades to come. This period of life offers both the most profound opportunities for life change and the greatest prospect for personal and spiritual redirection.

The Barna Research Group of Ventura, California, states that more than 70 percent of American adults had a period of time during their childhood when they regularly attended a Christian church. Six out of ten claim to attend church regularly, while four in five of those not exposed to church do not participate in organized religion.[4] A negative trend is visible in attendance among those exposed to church early on in life, however. While more than two thirds of those fifty-five and older who attended church as children still go to church, just over half of adults thirty-five and younger still go to church.[5]

George Barna, president of Barna Research, claims his group's findings show that one's church experience as a child is a much greater predictor of future church attendance than a parent's desire for their children to have a faith experience.[6] One challenge, then, is to reach a generation whose children, more than prior generations in America, are not experiencing church during these formative years. Without these positive associations with church, the chances of reintroducing today's children to church a decade or two from now becomes increasingly difficult.

Another challenge is to reach out in a gesture of healing and reconciliation to those who have been either hurt or neglected by church in the past. Without a new vision of what church can be, churches not only lose these young adults, but we also lose their children. Without a childhood experience in church, they are less likely to return as adults, and the cycle continues.

Our intention is not to discard all the church has offered so far. On the contrary, we hope on some level to reintroduce many fundamental tenets on which the original Christian movement was founded at Pentecost and during Jesus' own ministry. Timeless yet fundamental experiences such as sharing personal narratives and openness to the spontaneous sacred can be lacking in a more proscriptive, program-centered, institutionally-minded church. While church leaders should better understand the generation they are seeking to reach, they should also understand that the world does not need the church simply to reflect the world around it; instead, it needs the church to remain set apart, in the world, yet not entirely of it. At the same time, tomorrow's church must overcome some of its own hang-ups on institutional trappings, imagining church as only taking place at a certain time and in a certain place.

The irony of twenty-first-century ministry is that the church will find its relevance not in reflecting the culture around it, but in transcending it, offering something that extends back thousands of years, tapping into the needs of human nature. In a world of ever-increasing abstraction, mired in a flood of data irrespective of the quality of content, the church must be the catalyst that allows for sacred space wherever and whenever two or more gather to seek it. While we as church leaders must take the first step toward reconciliation with those who have left the church, we must not abandon the history and ritual that helps us understand our own corporate story as Christians. We are not just the church of the twenty-first century; we also are a church with history, a story to tell to those who are ready to listen. How, when, and where we tell it may look different, but the good news of the gospel is still the same.

The church that understands the present culture, while also embracing its own historical culture and story, lays the foundation for a future vision of hope and transformation. This book is only one perspective on an increasingly complex and ever-changing global culture. Today's church leaders find as many relevant experiences and educational opportunities outside the church and beyond books, engaging people on their own terms, listening before evangelizing, serving before inviting, and developing face-to-face community before focusing on a worship experience. Our stories are bound by the temporal and spatial contexts in which we live, but the ritual of sharing stories is timeless and crosses all cultural boundaries.

In connecting through our stories, we come to know each other in a sacred way, glimpsing the God of one another's understanding, if only for a moment. In these spontaneously sacred moments, we commune both with God and with each another in a way that, like the experience of the culture we seek to reach, extends beyond this time and place. We glimpse the infinite, the possible, and the beauty of God's infinite creation. From here, we can build a community of faith together that will nurture, serve, and encourage others and that will change the world.

About Our Research

We spent some time discussing how we wanted to gather information for this book. Much of what we read about young adults, particularly in theological books, is anecdotal and general in nature, while not including much firsthand information. As we believe that personal narrative is a central dynamic in the modern faith experience, we felt we ought to share as many stories as possible. Because of this, each chapter includes the story of an individual or couple that represents a different cross section of today's young adult population. Some have participated in organized religion their entire lives, while others came to church later in life. Some do not currently consider themselves religious, in that they do not regularly participate in any church activities. We asked them to share their understanding of faith, as well as offer a perspective about churches, denominations, and organized religion as a whole, from the outside, so to speak.

One of our concerns was confining people's experience within our own framework through predetermined questions or interview styles. Instead, we opted for a more unstructured documentary-style process for gathering stories. With the support of several churches in Texas and Colorado, we purchased five video cameras, which we then sent to people across the country. We gave them general guidelines about the ultimate purpose of the project and asked them to take about a week to record their stories in whatever way they felt appropriate.

Some participants sat in front of the cameras and relayed their faith experience in first person, while others interviewed other individuals and small groups about their opinions. The honesty with which people participated in this qualitative approach to research was refreshing and at times surprising. The stories and perspectives we witnessed throughout the project were deeply personal, thoughtful, and wide-ranging in their theological perspectives.

For those seeking a more straightforward guidebook about how to recruit and retain young adults in their church, this narrative style may prove frustrating at times. However, for those interested in better understanding the minds of today's young adults within a context of spiritual experience, we believe allowing others to tell their own stories in their own ways is the richest opportunity for growth in our collective understanding. After all, if adding numbers to our church rosters was as simple as outlining a few simple how-tos, that book would have already been written and would likely hit the bestseller list in a matter of weeks.

While we recognize the value of this sort of qualitative research, we also felt we ought to gather data on a broader scale and in more concrete, quantifiable terms. In this spirit, we conducted a comprehensive young adult spirituality survey online, asking fifty-seven questions about everything from personal religious affiliation to images of God, responsibility of the church in today's world, and the best and worst that organized religion presents. In just over two months, more than 750 people took part in the survey, yielding a rich and compelling story in itself. We will share this data throughout the book as appropriate, and we also have included a full presentation of the data for your own consideration on our Web site at www. christianpiatt.com.

Finally, we have made an effort to survey a reasonable sampling of literature and other research about contemporary spirituality and religious identity to offer a broader context within which to present our own findings. We are pleased to have a copy of the Baylor Religion Survey's report, titled *American Piety in the 21st Century: New Insights to the Depth and Complexity of Religion in the U.S.,* which was published in September 2006. This study, considered the most thorough and comprehensive study of American religious identity in history, surveyed more than 1,700 people about a broad range of theological, social, and moral issues. The opportunity to hold up our own data next to such a richly compiled scientific study gives added dimensions to our own work.

While we try to share practical ideas about ministry wherever possible, we believe it is much more important to provide an accurate and honest portrayal of young adult spiritual attitudes. We also feel strongly that no program or worship style can take the place of the bond formed through personal relationships, and that this bond takes place when two or more people engage in intentional, thoughtful, and constructive conversation. If nothing else, our hope is that this book creates more opportunities for such dialogue, helping to deepen the understanding among those both within and outside organized religious systems.

On the part of religious leadership, participating in this dialogue often requires openness to new interpretations of spirituality and a willingness to first discover the spiritual story of others rather than imparting one's own traditions and values. Whereas the church historically has served as the gateway to spiritual enlightenment for centuries, it now finds itself in the roles of partner and guide, growing alongside those seeking personal truth. All the while, we must maintain a meaningful connection with our collective spiritual history, learning from our theological ancestors, always setting time and space aside for shared experiences of the sacred.

Despite a recent trend toward custom-tailored social networks and a voracious appetite for instant access to information, we human creatures crave deep interpersonal relationships that challenge us to find deeper significance in the universe around us. Though we approach this journey with different traditions, different vocabularies to describe our understanding of God, and different levels of trust in the institution of church, the questions to which we ultimately seek answers are fundamentally similar. As we explore these deeply personal questions together, we make room for sacred moments, wherever we are, bonded by the unbreakable connection of the divine grace that holds the world together.

I Love to Tell the Story

We had the remarkable opportunity in 2006 to spend two days with Fred Craddock in a preaching workshop. Celebrated as one of the greatest preachers and storytellers of the modern Mainline church, we were willing repositories for his wisdom, intellect, and vision for what the church could still become.

It may seem strange that a seventy-eight-year-old man has his finger on the pulse of the church's future. Craddock claims that Christian life is an exercise in memory. This includes both individual and collective, historically based memory. Without this sense of memory, he says, we are nothing but orphans. We lack a sense of heritage and belonging, and a context any greater than our direct personal experience is absent. Historical, cultural, and ultimately theological myopia begins to settle in, resulting in a diminished sense of connectedness and no concept of greater cause and effect of one's life on the universe.

Another way, he says, to describe a generation seemingly set adrift within a boundaryless cultural landscape is to say that young adults lack a metanarrative. In general, we want for an internal story with which we identify and which helps inform and contextualize the future, along with inhering meaning to remembered experience.

Craddock offers four characteristics that help characterize an individual or group of people who lack such a metanarrative:

Low Expectations

Today's young adults sometimes are called the "so what" or "whatever" generation. We are characterized by a pervasive sense of apathy, skepticism, or even cynicism. From the inside, we recognize a multidimensional perspective of the world around us. Many of our peers share a unique combination of detached idealism, along with a distinct institutional suspicion. Although we are wary of any formally organized system for the most part, we still believe in the inherent goodness of people. Though the political and religious systems we have grown up in seem to be rife with scandal on a regular basis, we are unwilling in general to transfer our institutional skepticism to the individual level.

To be a skeptical idealist seems dichotomous, but one must consider the environment in which we formed our understanding, and subsequent values, about institutions of power. We have seen the highly divisive rifts over Vietnam and now Iraq. We watched some of the largest corporate flagships crumble to ruin and ridicule amid widespread scandal. Church leaders have been accused of everything from misappropriation of funds to gross sexual misconduct, and with every fallen leader, more people's confidence in religion as a whole is shaken.

From a more positive perspective, we have seen revolutionary voices such as Martin Luther King Jr. set a new course for equality. We continue to experience growing gender parity in many sectors, both public and private. However, that such changes were necessary suggests an underlying dynamic built upon oppression, inequity, and abuse of power. Many of us now see figures such as Christopher Columbus not as heroic explorers but as symbols of European imperialism, leading to the savage slaying and enslavement of millions of indigenous peoples. In embracing the hopeful vision of such leaders as Dr. King, we also must acknowledge a heritage of bigotry, hatred, and suffering.

With such evidence laid before our feet, people could easily conclude that modern society is dissolving toward a hopelessly tragic end. We must consider, however, that in the past, ignorance has also meant bliss in many cases. Just because people didn't hear about scandals such as Watergate before the dawn of the Information Age does not mean they didn't take place. Tens of thousands of people have been abused at the hands of figures of power, but a video clip of Rodney King being beaten on the side of the road brings police brutality to the forefront of the public consciousness within hours of the incident.

Public figures, along with all of their behavior, are increasingly scrutinized thanks to the overwhelming volume of—and immediate access to–information. Craddock tells a story that illustrates this point. Two boys were in a car that was struck by an oncoming train as they attempted to cross some poorly marked tracks. One boy died while the other lost both of his legs, and both families subsequently sued the railroad company for negligence. Though the jury awarded $3 million to the family of the injured young man, the family whose son died received nothing. The difference was that, though the second family's loss was greater, the jury could see the young man missing his legs, which had a more profound effect on their decision making than did more abstract stories about the boy who was no longer there.

Vivid images of scandal, violence, and abuse pouring into our living rooms have a profound impact on our understanding of reality and the systems that govern the world. Such information infects our innocence at increasingly younger ages, also leading to parenting intent on sheltering children from the evils of the world that seem imminently present. Our social context begins to feel morally flexible, if not void, and we learn to live more out of a reactive fear than a compelling sense of hopefulness. The world seems messy, chaotic, and perilously close to self-destruction. Then we have the church, whose ritual and traditions convey a sense of symmetry and timelessness that feels grossly out of touch with the world around it.

As preservers of an abstract sense of history, the church risks a growing perception of obsolescence. As champions on the forefront of an ever-present struggle for social justice and compassion for the marginalized, however, the church has its greatest opportunity to make real the mission of the gospel to a world that longs for a glimmer of hope, realized in the actions of those committed to Christlike service. Craddock claims the job of the church is to make that which is absent become present for those who seek hope in the church. Later in this chapter, we consider some ways in which both stories and mission-centered activism can tap into the latent idealism of a generation thirsting for a future that is different from what they see on their televisions and computer screens.

Retreat

Mitigation of risk has become a driving force in modern American culture, for good reason in some cases. We're a litigious, lawsuit-happy society, bent on getting what we "deserve" any time we feel we have suffered injustice. From zero-tolerance judicial systems to booming personal, local, and national security industries, we have become intent on extracting risk from our surroundings. If this is not possible, we extricate ourselves, isolating our loved ones in a protective bubble.

The explosive popularity of homeschooling is another example of this desire to protect children from the world. With every event such as the Columbine High School shootings, the desire to develop a custom-tailored, self-centered community grows. The perceived danger of community means that presence and physical community have given way to anonymity and abstraction. This large-scale withdrawal from traditional social circles results in a more disparate, decentralized "para-community."

Despite this tendency toward social retreat, we are still social creatures by nature. For many, technology has developed to a point that it can fill this void, though not entirely in the way we have interacted historically. MySpace is a perfect example. In a few short years, this social networking Web site has grown to accommodate more than *140 million* members. Features of the site are highly customizable, enabling users to reflect much about their own personalities in their page. First, members choose a username that can either be their given name or some other pseudonym that reflects something about their persona to the MySpace community.

Though we use our pages primarily to share information about various projects, a majority of users simply employ MySpace as a social networking tool. Each page includes the capability for personalized designs, photo albums, blogs,[1] biographical information, calendars and other indicators about the unique personality of the user.

The veracity of information on MySpace pages is always questionable. Some even use the site to role-play, developing personas from television shows and movies. They then invite one another to online "parties," where they take on their virtual alter egos and interact as if they were fictional characters such as those from Harry Potter, the television show *Lost,* or even figures from comic books. At this level, the sense of removal is so great that the user's identity is completely irrelevant, subsumed by a fantasy constructed in the imagination of the user.

Virtual communities have benefits and drawbacks. On the positive side, they provide an opportunity for people from a broad spectrum of backgrounds to find one another and to create an online community. Christian has "friends" on his MySpace page from all over the country, as well as the United Kingdom, Poland, and even the Philippines. Digital communication breaks down many hierarchic strangleholds on many types of data, from music and books to film. Many authors and artists have found venues for their work online with minimal investment. Of course, with the ease of production and distribution of information comes the potential for the dilution of quality. One may have to sift through hundreds of independent musicians to find something one considers to be of quality, but the power to choose lies in users' own hands, to the degree that they are willing to invest the time and effort.

Unfortunately, most of us don't have the time or patience to wade through a virtual sea of data to pluck out a unique morsel that tickles our fancy. This is why online giants such as America Online, MSN, and Yahoo! are in business. By collecting personal data about each user, they can present a tailor-made Web experience and save users the effort of having to seek out what they want. This, in turn, closely mirrors the more traditional corporate environment to which we have been accustomed, despite utopian predictions that the Internet would bring commercial superpowers to their knees.

Though young adults have a unique social outlet with online venues such as MySpace, these Web sites also have the potential to dilute the human experience. Face-to-face communication gives way to text messaging, chat rooms, and online special interest groups. Interpersonal experience becomes more abstracted, and hence, further removed from the innate biological need we have to connect with people physically, emotionally, and spiritually. In some ways we settle for attenuated interpersonal practices in exchange for personal choice and a broadly diverse population of potential acquaintances.

Another contribution to the retreat effect lies in the sheer volume of data itself. Abraham Lincoln told the story of walking miles to the local library. He, and others of his period, had to aggressively seek information, and they often had to settle for whatever they could find. Today, global search engines, digital journal subscriptions, and online libraries place more information at the tips of our fingers than we ever could digest in ten lifetimes. Rather than being proactive seekers of information, we become more passive filters of the flood of data streaming toward us in a never-ending onslaught. This onslaught contributes to the "lean-back" effect, as Craddock calls it. We long to get away from it all, finding welcome relief when we escape beyond the reach of mobile phones and e-mail.

Somehow we're also terribly dependent on that which we've come to resent. Christian's job is a good example. As a nonprofit consultant, columnist, and author, he can work from anywhere. This flexibility allows him to work from home, affording him more time with his family and for their church's ministry. However, the advent of the same technology that has allowed this freedom also raises expectations. To some degree, we are expected to be available day and night, regardless of where we are.

With the efficiencies of technology, some people expected that workweeks would shrink. On the contrary, performance expectations have risen to fill the void, contributing even more pressure to the schedules of a digitally-bound employee. At times, the digital revolution, which promised to free us from the chains of physical offices, has become a highly mobile yoke we bear at all times. Such added pressures and expectations feed the desire to escape and withdraw, while at the same time, today's average young adult feels strangely naked or rudderless without the electronic umbilical cord.

Loss of Absolutes

If "peace, love, and rock and roll" was the definitive catchphrase of the parents of today's young adults, our equivalent calling card arguably would be, "celebrate diversity." The pluralism of modern America is more prominent and broadly accepted than ever before. This pluralism does not come without growing pains and consequences, however. As people challenge and reinvent established norms, traditions, and systems, they experience an ongoing sense of displacement, dynamic a-centricity, and sometimes a disconcertingly pervasive feeling of relativism. Today's debates about immigration speak to the struggles to find a point of balance within which the multitude of cultures and traditions can coexist without anyone feeling compromised, devalued, or abused.

Craddock notes that pluralism introduces a heightened sense of the "other." A more homogenous environment allows people to feel they are part of a greater whole, to the point that much of what defines them as individuals is effectively taken for granted. Our uniqueness rises to the surface in contexts where we find ourselves next to someone unlike ourselves. We become more sensitive to differences, recognizing in more situations that the way we may have once assumed the world worked does not exactly apply to everyone else. We like to call this the disintegration of the cultural snow globe effect.

While our own experience can be greatly enriched by being introduced to the beliefs, traditions, and experiences of others unlike us, this diversity also challenges the sense of consistency and predictability for which we all long in order to feel confident and safe. A "normal" way of operating no longer exists. We become aware of our own smallness and relatively biased outlook on the world. We are much more aware of our economic status, our cultural identity (though we may know little at all about our cultural history), and the stereotypes in which we tend to live and those which we may consciously or unconsciously challenge.

We see the effects of this pluralism within Mainline Christian churches. Though Anglos have traditionally held the majority of positions of leadership, racial/ethnic constituencies are the fastest growing subsections of the Christian Church (Disciples of Christ). People try to incorporate and understand one another's traditions, but we all are understandably reluctant to abandon our own way of doing things. In addition to differences in worship styles, Christians have fundamental differences in theological values and even God imagery, in many cases. Though we may value and even celebrate our differences within a culturally diversifying church body, we hardly understand one another's faith.

Today's young adults face an identity crisis deeply rooted in all the cultural, moral, and religious systems around them. In our plurality, we have yet to understand who we are collectively. In some cases, this leads to resistance to change, and in others, it manifests itself as a self-effacing, almost shame-filled image of one's self.

Christian is involved with the Disciples' Leadership Institute (DLI), a program of the Christian Church (Disciples of Christ) Higher Education Leadership Ministry office. DLI brings together a culturally diverse cross section of young lay ministry leaders and clergy to engage in dialogue and practice that they hope will lead to a stronger future for the church. During the weeklong retreats, worship teams take turns planning daily worship services. The first year, this was done by ethnic tradition, offering a traditionally African American service one evening, a Caribbean service the next, and so on.

The Anglo worship was to take place the final morning before everyone returned home, and a curious trend developed over the course of the week. Those involved with the Anglo worship planning spoke in self-deprecating terms, warning people about the "boring white worship" looming on Friday. Eventually the group confronted us about this, challenging us to take pride in our own traditions and to stop apologizing for who we were.

Honestly, this self-deprecation has become a habit among many young white Americans, particularly males. In countless situations, people tell jokes about males or white people that would not be considered appropriate if the subject belonged to a different group. White males hold most of the power in America, and even as values and power shift, the white male is an easy target in some ways for teasing, both externally and from within our own ranks. It's almost as if we white males feel we should apologize in advance for being who we are, lest we offend someone with our very existence.

Of course, the identity crisis is not only borne by white males. On the contrary, we all live in a sort of liminal state, wanting to break free from white male systems of power, yet not fully embracing a new, pluralistic paradigm. This leads to intense self-awareness and even self-doubt. Being so aware of one's differences is uncomfortable, but it is also a necessary by-product of growing into a more pluralistic American future vision.

A Sense of Mystery

The Information Age has placed our body of knowledge within a new, significantly greater context. With instant access to so much information, we become increasingly aware of how much we don't know. By necessity, our respective knowledge bases become ever narrower and more specialized, further weakening the social fabric, as we have less common knowledge, compared with our dedicated areas of experience. What we have most in common is a shared sense of the vastness of the unknown.

Familiar ground based on an apparent negative may seem a curious opportunity, but within this sense of awe, mystery, and relative smallness young adults can find an occasion for a collective mood of reverence. Within this humbling framework we can avail ourselves of an encounter with God.

The Baylor Institute for Studies of Religion survey, published in September 2006,[2] notes that although 85 to 90 percent of Americans claim to believe in God and 82 percent claim to be Christians, a surprisingly rich and complex diversity of religious views lies just below the surface when individuals are questioned about their spiritual beliefs. Though a vast majority of Americans pray at least once a week, "they do not agree about what God is like, what God wants for the world, or how God feels about politics."[3] Though young adults are less likely to identify with a particular denomination or religious tradition, a sense of mysticism, including belief in the paranormal, is greatest among people age eighteen to thirty, steadily decreasing with each respective age category.

If one perceives the mission of the church to be one of conforming the world to an established set of creeds or proscriptive beliefs, such pluralistic and mystical trends may prove disturbing. However, if one sees openness to an experience of transcendence as a door through which the church may enter into dialogue, today's young adults offer a fresh landscape. We often are filled with spiritual curiosity and interest in communion with something greater than ourselves, while also being resistant in many ways to dogma, and even denominational affiliation.

The institution of church as it is historically understood holds less value for American young adults, while spiritual curiosity remains surprisingly strong. It is the church, then, that finds itself at a crossroads, forced to choose whether its traditional structures and creeds are more important than the opportunity to reach out to people where they are. For those willing to share in this sense of mystery and awe, the religious future of America is exciting and filled with possibility. For those whose focus is preservation of a certain set of practices or traditions, the growing rejection of denominations and dogma is a threat to their way of life.

Amy's Story

Loneliness is one of my worst fears. It comes from way, way back as worst fears usually do. It's not being alone with myself that I mind as much as being left by others. That's where I lose it. I learned what that was like when I was three years old. My parents divorced just a few months after my third birthday. The fighting was futile, but they did it anyway.

I stayed in my room. The yelling kept me there. It wasn't until it got quiet that I popped my head out in the hallway, just in time to catch sight of my mom grabbing my baby brother and heading out the door. My dad broke down and cried–something I'd never seen before. I needed him to hold it together, but he could no more suppress his tears than he could turn down a shot of whiskey. So, he did what he knew. He clutched his keys and started for the liquor store. As he was closing the door behind him, I finally spoke up.

"Dad, where are you going?" I knew, but I asked anyway.

His face dripped with shame. Reality does that to addicts. To this day I can spot shame on an addict's face from a hundred paces.

He thought my mom had taken me with her.

"Where are you going?" I asked again. He was in a hurry. That scared me even more. That's the first time I remember feeling the sense of urgency that has nipped at my heels ever since: "Hurry! Hurry! You don't have much time. You'd better go!" Now it's a familiar annoyance. Then, it was an earthquake.

He grabbed a footstool and placed it in the front hall. He squatted down next to it and patted it with his hand, motioning me to come and sit down.

Good, comfort. That's what I need, I thought. I ran over and sat next to him.

"Can you count to a hundred?" he asked me. I nodded. Counting was not comforting, and I couldn't even count to twenty, which he knew, but I told him I could because I wanted to make him feel better. In that moment the first hints of codependency crept in. *I was only three.*

"Good. Sit here and count to a hundred, and I'll be back before you're done."

"OK" I said. I was so compliant, a trait that would get lost in adolescence.

Then he left.

I could go on about how he should have taken me along. I could have waited in the car or even gone in the liquor store with him. But that's not what happened, and that's not the point.

I was left alone. And I didn't know for how long.

In that moment, I believed I had lost my family forever. In a way I had. In a few weeks the papers were filed and the proceedings began, along with the arguments about album collections and fine china.

For all I knew, at that moment, I was on my own. Fear can often be traced back to formative days like that day.

I sat on the little stool, lips quivering with each number. As I counted aloud, I remember trying to imagine how I was going to take care of the house and myself. It was a prayer of sorts—a chant. It helped keep me calm.

Looking back, I can see how hard I've fought to avoid being left alone. I've put up with a lot of cruelty and abuse too. *Anything's better than being left.*

Only in recent years have I begun to realize a couple of things: There are far worse things than being left, and God does not leave.

I still wrestle with the demons of loneliness. I still lose sleep worrying about my family and what will happen, not if, but when they leave, by way of death or other means.

Despite all of the worrying, so much good can and does happen. My dad celebrated nineteen years of sobriety this year. There has been more joy than anything in my life. I owe that to God, to church, and to twelve-step groups.

Anne Lamott wrote an article about her teenage son, Sam. She admits she makes him go to church with her because she can. That's pretty much how it was for me. My dad was, and is, a minister. I had to go to church. Thank God. Lamott says kids need to go to church because they "get to meet some of the people who love God back. Learning to love back is the hardest part of being alive."[4] Amen.

I have known a lot of people who love God back. Marie was my church camp counselor when I was in junior high school. That's about the time the compliance of my childhood disappeared. I was angry, confused, and hormonal. Marie was Jesus in the form of a fortysomething, large-breasted, boisterous hug. She hugged me every time she saw me. When I sobbed uncontrollably on those large breasts for what seemed like hours, she just kept on hugging me. That's church.

I have never told Marie how much I love her. I need to. She is one of the reasons I decided to go into ministry. If the love of God could come through her, it could come through me too—breasts and all. That's what she taught me. I didn't think breasts would be a problem, but for some people, they are. To this day I still get comments like,

"That was a pretty good sermon…for a woman." I'm not sure what that means, but I think it has something to do with breasts.

When I chose a robe for my ordination, I couldn't help but notice that none of them was particularly flattering to a woman's figure. It's not that they are supposed to be sexy, or even shapely, but they are completely devoid of any hint of the female form. That saddened me. I am an embodiment of the love of Jesus Christ. Marie taught me that. She would have filled up my robe, but it just hangs on me. My friends call it the "Darth Maul" robe. That's the bad guy from *Star Wars Episode 1: The Phantom Menace.* That wasn't really the look I was going for, but it's empowering nonetheless, I suppose.

Empowerment is the work that we need to be about in the world. My first sermon was for a youth Sunday when I was in eighth grade. It sucked. What had been an eight-minute sermon at home became a ninety-second race in the pulpit. I remember quoting Martin Luther King, Jr. That was probably the only redeeming element of the whole thing, but the whole church came and hugged me and told me how proud of me they were that day. They didn't lie. They didn't say it was a good sermon, but they empowered me. They saw a spark and they fanned the flame, when they could have just as easily hidden me under a bushel.

It did not even occur to me that, as a woman, I would not be readily accepted in a pastoral role. I was just Amy, a girl who was loved into ministry. I didn't meet a female minister until I was a teenager. Listening to her was different, not because of the breasts, but her voice was so much higher than my father's. His was the voice I'd heard most of my life. Then there was my grandfather and my great-grandfather; they were all preachers too. I come from a long line of preachers. It's in my blood. I thought it was a curse for a long time. Afflictions at some point either become the source of our demise or our strength. Like Paul, if we can surrender to them, we find new vision and hope. If we fight against them, they bring us to our knees. If we surrender, we end up on our knees. Either way, we don't have control, and kneeling before God is a good place to be.

Not until I got to seminary did I begin to appreciate my family's curse. I am, in the truest sense of the term, a WASP (White Anglo-Saxon Protestant). After digging through some genealogical records, I discovered that the most I am of any one heritage is one-eighth Swedish. How's that for a mutt? I was jealous of my friends with "real" roots—an ancestry to be proud of, something that defines them and shapes their identity in the world.

Romantic? Yes. Unrealistic? Of course. But when they sit down to fill out an employment application they get to check a box that means something. I check a box next to the word "White." What does that mean?

I am a white girl from Colorado. I have come to terms with that. At least I can dance, and I speak pretty decent Spanish, but I'm white. "White" means privilege—unbelievable privilege. It means power and influence, opportunity and preference, oppression and hatred. I have to accept these as well. I am a product of, beneficiary of, and reaction to all these things, but what lies beyond? I found the answer once again at church.

My great-grandfather started churches in both Wyoming and Colorado. I have relatives in the cemetery near Cane Ridge, the site of one of the greatest religious revivals in American history. My grandparents on my mother's side have dedicated their entire lives to ministry and service. My father has as well. These are my roots. My story is the church's story. In finally coming to terms with this reality, I was able to commit myself wholly to a life of ministry. In order to know who I am, I have to *be* who I am—a church girl.

Does that mean I wear my Darth Maul robe everywhere? No. Does it mean that I always represent the church at its best, or that I am the only version of church out there? Not even close. But I am Amy: child of God, church girl, dancer, white girl. The more comfortable I become with myself, the easier it is to accept others. Church should help people to know who they are. Stories are the best way we have of sharing this knowledge. Jesus liked stories. He knew that we would remember those better than genealogies or lectures. Everyone has a story to tell, and we can all be a part of the church's story.

If, as I stated earlier, there are far worse things than being left, and God doesn't leave, then church is a place where people should stay. Why, then, have so many left? We are a covenant people with a holy promise to God and to one another. We are not supposed to leave, but we do all the time. This is a source of both pain and confusion for me.

One of the most important parts of my job involves making sure everyone has a place at Christ's table. Each week when I break the bread and give the words of institution, I remind the people as well as myself that it is an open table. "There is always room for one more," I say. At that point, I force myself to picture the "one" in my life who I'd like least to have to sit with and mentally pull out a chair for him or her. Then, and only then, can I find my seat. It's a silly exercise, but it helps make communion real for me.

How, then, can people so quickly get up and leave the table? Do they not realize how difficult it can be to set their place? Do they have any idea how heavy that chair is for me to lift or how tightly cramped I feel when they first sit down? I take all of this personally, though usually it has little to do with me.

Sometimes people leave for what they consider to be good reasons: They get a job somewhere else; they feel called to another community. I can live with that. But the very human sense of betrayal is personally difficult to overcome as a pastor. Whether that sense is because of addiction, fear, or abuse, it is always hard to accept, and the result is always the same: pain.

There is justifiable pain, and there is needless suffering. I think people confuse the two. People believe that when they leave a church, they are not leaving God. Spirituality has become so individualistic that we assume church is not something that happens in community so much as it does within our hearts. Conversely, the church is guilty of the notion that salvation can only happen within its walls. Craddock says we serve a God that is "both/and." We try to make life "either/or," and God is constantly calling us to open our hearts and minds to see more truth.

God is both community and individual, personal and shared. Many of my "secular" friends–they laugh when I call them that–say their church is on a mountaintop or in a good book. Fine, I say. But what about when chaos ensues or tragedy occurs? Can a mountain come to you in the hospital, weep over your loss, break bread with you, pray for you, or pull out a chair when you need to sit and rest and be fed? Can a book love you back? We all need someone to love us back.

If today's church can find sincere ways to love people, not just *like* them, then we will begin to heed the call of Christ: to be the one who can look a stranger in the eye and say "I give my life for you." If we are offering anything less we are falling short, we are phonies, and people will see it and walk on by. Small groups have their place. Programs that appeal to every age group and demographic are fine too, but they are not life-giving.

In some ways, the concept is so simple that we overlook it. Hear this: It is simple, but not easy, to give our very selves away in the name of love. Something as simple as hugging a sad little girl, loving her despite her adolescent inadequacies, letting her cry, and never leaving her alone can give her enough life to want to give it away to others. It worked for me.

An Overarching Purpose

The invitation to church is "Come and hear the story. Come and share your story. Together, we are a shared story." Participants are asked to "try on" the various perspectives and narratives of others. Much like Alcoholics Anonymous, the appeal is to "take what you like and leave the rest."[5] This is the greatest appeal of the Disciples of Christ church in the twenty-first century. As a creedless system, we have no official dogma that individuals must adhere to in order to participate fully. For some, the lack of formal structure is unsettling. When asked what Disciples stand for or what a Disciples church is like, a few generalities apply in most cases. Together, members claim to have no creed beyond a shared love of Christ. Beyond this we take three defining positions: in essentials, unity; in nonessentials, liberty; in all things, charity/love.

One of the greatest criticisms of our denomination is that we do not tell people what to do or how to be. For those who find the aforementioned lack of absolutes as a crisis of religious identity, Disciples offer little comfort with respect to boundaries of propriety.

As much as some young adults gravitate toward such a creedless, nonhierarchic system, an equally strong contingency from this generation adheres to more strict traditions. The Baylor study discovered that fully one third (33.6 percent) of all Americans, 100 million people, identify themselves as affiliated with the Evangelical Protestant tradition.[6] Though those persons surveyed in the Baylor study aged eighteen to thirty were three times more likely to have no religious affiliation than those over the age of sixty-five, they also are the most likely of any age group to identify themselves as Evangelicals.

In such a polarized religious climate, how does the church reach out as a voice of reconciliation and healing? First, we must reenvision what it means to be church. When asked how many Christian churches are in our community, the answer should be "one." If a family leaves our church for another, our focus should not be on the loss, but rather on the recognition that our particular faith community cannot, and should not, be all things for all people. We must place our passionate commitment to gospel-centered ministry and Christlike service before concerns about budgets, buildings, and salaries. After all, the Christian faith is not an institution: it is a movement. We would do well to better understand our own relative importance within the context of the human faith experience.

Perhaps most important, and at the heart of our reconciliation efforts, is offering an overarching purpose for those who seek it. With the disintegration of the nuclear family, geographically dispersed relatives, and ever-higher degrees of mobility, we tend to lack a sense of place and purpose. Our identity is more beholden to our achievements and career status than our familial, cultural, or religious heritage. This makes for a tenuous and fragile foundation upon which to build one's concept of self. As Craddock says, without our own metanarrative, we are nothing but orphans.

Through stories, we develop such an internal narrative. Through stories, we develop an identity richer and deeper than the present. Through stories, we connect with one another in the meaningful ways for which we long, and for which we are biologically hardwired.[7] Stories are the means by which we understand our history as Christians. Jesus chose to share his message of good news with the world through stories. In learning to formulate and share our stories with one another we develop our overarching purpose, both individually and collectively.

Faith is a journey through life rather than a destination at which one arrives with complete answers and wholeness. Instead, God is what makes us whole. Without God, we are not whole. As the Psalmist laments in Psalm 42, "so my soul longs for you, O God. My soul thirsts for God, for the living God. When shall I come and behold the face of God?"[8] Like Jesus from the cross, we cry out "I am thirsty."[9] Our longing for God is what draws us to one another and to sharing our stories.

Church can provide a safe and welcoming place for people to share, hear, embrace, heal, question, and discern stories. Throughout history, human beings have used stories to "explore the fundamental mysteries: *Who are we? Why are we? How are we to live?*"[10] At their best, stories bring to life the shared human experience. In sharing our truths, we share God with one another and build a loving community.

We may not quench our thirst entirely, but we supply one another with drink for the journey.

Without both the cultivation of a shared story and the opportunity to share our individual stories, we risk sterilization and immobility as a church. As Carl Jung states, "one of the main functions of formalized religion is to protect people against a direct experience of God."[11] Here, the value of story becomes evident: without it, we cannot connect. Our claim is not to have the corner on truth, per se, but to a path that leads to hope and an open-ended future. Insofar as the church does not live out this call, we fulfill Jung's claim, becoming a roadblock for meaningful spiritual experience rather than facilitating it.

In a time when so many in the religious community are claiming ultimate truth and absolute assuredness, we can instead offer a vision of possibility and liberation. The collective wonder that stories provide and the shared beauty of experience are fertile soil that, over time, will yield great fruit. Even stories of rejection, failure, and tragedy can be transformed into abundant sources of life. If even Jesus cried out, then so can we. Ours is the story of a savior who was tortured and left for dead. It is his thirst with which we can identify. We too know what it is to thirst, to have a longing from deep within. This is a story worth sharing, an invitation worth accepting.

Other considerations about the importance of story include the following:

- It is the context in which we can relate to scripture today.
- It helps us get beyond superficial identities and stereotypes of one another.
- No one can argue with someone else's stories, whereas starting with ideas is potentially divisive.
- It taps into a critically fundamental part of ourselves that we fail to access much of the time.
- It gives us a compelling reason to come together, because sharing stories face-to-face is part of our nature.
- Though stories can serve as the foundation for postmodern ministry, they also are primitive, which makes them immune to trends and clichés.
- Once we know one another's stories, we start to build a collective story for the church, our families, and community.

Stories, as part of Bible study and sermon delivery, are pretty well a given. However, engaging others in articulating and sharing their stories in a way that is deeply meaningful is more complex. In his book *Remembering the Future, Imagining the Past,* David Hogue says that "our brains are created, or have evolved, to make meaning out of our experiences."[12] He also notes that not only do people yearn to make sense of the world, but we actually filter stories based on the degree to which they support or challenge our existing understanding of things and ourselves.

This understanding of ourselves can have both negative and positive consequences. For example, if we identify ourselves as perpetual victims, the stories with which we may identify more may be those which further validate our victimhood. In doing so, these same stories occlude significant dimensions of our own personalities, distilling us down to a string of self-fulfilling prophecies. However, stories focused on personal and corporate healing, Hogue says, must walk a fine line between pragmatic portrayals of real life and images of what is possible:

> Healing calls for a balance between confronting the reality of limitations with hope for change, so that one's addictions or history of abuse do not become the center of one's identity.[13]

Stories, then, bring hope and healing by grounding us in the present, while also casting a vision of a future based on hope. All of this is contextualized by past experience, shared history, and stories of which we become an active part. In coming together, sharing stories of hope and healing within the context of faith, we become coauthors and cocreators in a still-evolving, divinely inspired creation that began with the Word, as told in the gospel of John.

This sort of creative dialogue can take place in many ways in a religious setting, but we have selected a few examples for practical illustrations. In our church, we have sought ways to involve people in sharing their personal stories in worship, but only a few were ever willing to step up and accept the challenge of being so vulnerably intimate. We needed something to help mediate the direct attention experienced during storytelling. So we went back to basics: show and tell.

The idea came from a project originally done at Evergreen Christian Church in northern Colorado. The congregation needed a new communion table, but they resolved that the table needed to communicate something unique about the nature of the church. For Disciples, the table is a central focus of worship because we observe communion every week. The church determined that each family should bring a piece of wood from something in their home that had special significance to them.

Some families brought portions of old banisters, while others took samples from family rocking chairs, old toys, and other artifacts. The pieces then were combined in mosaic patterns to compose the top of the table. In this way, the table itself was a metaphor, telling the story of those families who invested themselves in one another and the growth of the shared ministry.

The idea occurred to us: what if each person told the story of the piece of wood they brought for the table as it was put into place? Now, each week a different person brings something of significance to them that relates to the worship theme and shares a story about it at offering time. The object itself serves as an anchor to which we all can connect back to the story the person told. For the narrator, the attention of the congregation is displaced onto the object, rather than onto them. We have had more willing participants, and the exercise has helped make what has been an obligatory offering meditation time into a sacred shared moment.

As noted earlier in this chapter, Christian is involved with the Disciples Leadership Institute. At the first weeklong retreat in the summer of 2006, the group experimented with a number of communication formats. The best-received experience of the entire week was something most in attendance had not tried before. For approximately ten minutes, one person would share his or her own faith story. Surprisingly, the stories people shared were profoundly personal and deeply affecting. The group comprised a lot of ministers, most of whom have plenty of practice talking about themselves. However, the accounts were not told as sermons, but as personal accounts of rich, diverse, beautiful lives.

Following the testimony, a second person joined the storyteller, responding to what she or he heard by asking questions. Leaders established clear guidelines to ensure that people were not placed in uncomfortable situations. Questions were general in nature and geared toward opportunities for the entire group to learn something from that individual's experience. Amid all of the study, small group discussions, activities, and worship, this was by far the most important thing that most members of the group took home with them.

Finally, an inner city church in Denver has looked for creative new ways to connect with the highly eclectic community just beyond its doors. As membership continued to age and dwindle in numbers, those inside the church clearly did not reflect those on the other side of the walls. In the middle of a burgeoning metropolitan arts community sits an exquisite example of late nineteenth-century church architecture: a monument of inspired creation in itself.

Church leaders agreed that the sanctuary and fellowship hall could serve as a perfect gallery for local artists. However, they wanted to be intentional about the way they used the space, so they planned a pilot project to test the concept. For Easter in 2006, they recruited fifteen local artists (five from within the church and ten with no formal connection to the congregation) and asked each of them to present the fourteen Stations of the Cross[14] (two artists worked together on one station). Other members of the church contributed to create the necessary atmosphere for each piece, and artists were given great latitude in the way they interpreted each Station.

The installations included folk art, poetry, stained glass, a worship and communion station, multimedia, ceramics, and more. They invited the public to a gallery-style exhibit of the work, and the three-day exhibit from Maundy Thursday to Holy Saturday drew more than five hundred people. The event was so successful that the church now is working on converting a portion of its old education wing into an art incubator. In exchange for free studio space, local artists will commit to participating in a number of similar exhibits throughout the year.

Hogue claims that people who do not understand their own stories have no unique sense of self, and hence, no sense of continuity, with no connection between their present and the past. This in turn inhibits the ability to imagine a future, rendering them without a sense of direction or greater meaning beyond their immediate experience.[15] Story is a vehicle by which we connect one another's present reality, a meaningful past, and a hopeful future, and it should not be confined to the pages of a book or a few minutes behind the pulpit. It is a corporate experience, or else it loses its power. Story includes any mode of expression within which body and soul intersect. The soul in this case "communicates a sense of transcendent timelessness and embodied timelessness, of unity with the Other and unique personhood."[16]

In these sacred moments of intimate communion and sharing, the overwhelming awareness of the Other begins to give way to the unique personhood of each individual with whom we have such meaningful contact. Each person begins to be valued not for what they can do, but for who they are as part of God's inspired creation. In these spontaneously sacred moments, we are elevated beyond the constraints of time, able to envision what lies ahead of us, and to bring absent history to life in present consciousness. In these sacred moments, we plant the seeds of a spiritual family, and the longing for connection that we all seek to satisfy begins to find fulfillment.

The God Image

Lisa Higaki, age 24, lives in Los Angeles. In January 2007, she spoke with Judy Woodruff from the *The News Hour with Jim Lehrer* about her faith:

> "I don't think I've ever known a moment without God in my life," she says. "Not taking it as a religion, as something that's, like, just labeled on me, like, 'I'm Japanese-American. I'm a woman. I'm a daughter. I'm a sister.' But actually kind of like a lifestyle, in a sense. I mean, it's just been kind of, like, my personal kind of identity."[1]

Lisa claims her connection to Christianity in particular comes from her parents, though she personally does not feel as strong a connection to church as her family. "I don't think they've ever really pushed [religion] upon me," she explains. "I think it was always, it was kind of just part of growing up, growing up in the church."[2]

Referring to research conducted by the Barna Group, Woodruff points out that Lisa's lack of connection between her faith and organized religion is not uncommon. Barna found that 60 percent of people now in their twenties who were involved with church as teenagers are no longer affiliated with a church.

Baylor Institute for Studies of Religion's 2006 survey, completed in cooperation with the Gallup Organization, makes many claims, including: "Americans are losing a strong denominational identity," and Americans are "more likely to connect with religion at the local level."[3]

Despite arguments to the contrary, a vast majority of Americans today claim to believe in God (85–90 percent); more than four out of five Americans claim to identify themselves as Christians; and more than 70 percent pray at least once a week. Amid cries of growing secularism in American society, at the heart of American culture lies a deep, personal connection to God.

What we also see is increasingly decentralized identification with institutions of faith. Even those within particular denominations vary widely in their political positions, personal theology, interpretation of scripture, and concepts such as salvation and the role of the church in society. As connections with particular denominations weaken, bonds among people of faith tend to be based more upon common ideology than on a common religious culture or institutional history.

A Generation Adrift

In her book *A History of God,* Karen Armstrong speaks to the necessity for the variability of God images within Christianity, Judaism, and Islam in particular:

> There is no one unchanging idea contained in the word, 'God'; instead, the word contains a whole spectrum of meanings, some of which are contradictory or mutually exclusive. Had the notion of God not had this flexibility, it would not have survived.[4]

She goes on to refute the notion of an 'absolute' understanding of God:

> If we look at our three religions (Christianity, Islam and Judaism), it becomes clear that there is no objective view of 'God': each generation has to create the image of God that works for it.[5]

One identifying characteristic of today's young adults is that we are "a generation adrift." Even the ominously generic moniker of "Generation X" suggests a population without direction, identity, or, in the most judgmental cases, a sense of purpose. Part of this understanding of contemporary young adults arises from the aforementioned rejection en masse of institutional identities. Personal choice, sparked both by the fierce individualism of our parents and the customized environments afforded by technology, has superseded shared experience as the driving force of young adults.

It is no particular surprise, then, that we are equally pluralistic and personalized with respect to images of God.

If indeed the notion of disconnectedness for today's young adults is accurate, it may be helpful to consider the religious identity and experience of populations recently introduced to American culture. In this sense, new immigrants face the same issues as today's young Americans, including a lack of corporate identity, disconnection with the culture that surrounds them, and reinterpretation of religious archetypes in new and creative ways.

Sociologist Franklin Woo points out not only the inevitability, but the necessity of each generation to arrive at its own theological identity, distinct from its predecessors:

> The concept of God held by one generation might be meaningless to subsequent generations; these concepts need to change in order to be relevant to the felt needs of a people, or be discarded completely.[6]

This suggests that the church's concepts of God, as reflected in traditions, rituals, and even God images, must evolve with the culture or risk being rejected as irrelevant. Even worse, inflexible concepts of God translate as a repudiation of the values of the current generation, requiring them to conform to existing paradigms only, without bringing any of themselves to a more dialogic atmosphere in which everyone's understanding is enriched by a diversity of views.

Though such institutional rigidity can be pervasive, the adaptability and openness of some churches has created fertile ground, both for immigrants and for young adults. Though many may consider American Evangelical churches to be the most didactic and unbending in their theology, they actually are attracting these groups in much greater numbers than Mainline churches.[7] Consider this quote from Kenneth Guest's book, *God in Chinatown,* regarding recent Chinese immigrants from Fuzhou and their relationship to Evangelical Christianity:

> Outside they are exploited workers; inside they may be respected members and leaders of their church community. Outside they may be illegal immigrants, undocumented workers, invisible to the U.S. state or even targets of INS raids and crackdowns; inside they are children of God... Outside they are sinners, lawbreakers, one step away from

imprisonment and deportation, the truncation of their dreams of freedom, liberation, and financial success; inside they are exhorted to remember that while a U.S. green card may be nice, only God's green card will get them to heaven.[8]

With respect to young adults, this data bears out as well. While many perceive younger people to be more amoral and secular, the Baylor study yields surprising evidence to the contrary. Though people between the ages of eighteen and thirty indeed are much more likely not to identify with any religious tradition than any other age group, they are also the most likely to attend an Evangelical Protestant church.[9]

Woo points out that this is not a recent phenomenon, particularly with respect to immigrant communities. Research demonstrates that this appeal has existed within the Evangelical Christian tradition for decades:

> Sociologist Yang Fenggang (himself an immigrant to the United States), in his study of primarily middle-class Chinese Christians in the United States since the early 1950s, concludes that the Christian church (mostly evangelical conservative) is a social mechanism that enables Chinese new-comers to America both to selectively become Americans and to maintain their Chinese identity on their own terms.[10]

For a generation that identifies closely with this sort of disconnectedness and lack of group identity, it is no surprise that the same faith tradition has great appeal for many young adults. For some young Americans, however, issues such as conservative social values, literal interpretation of scripture, and the emphasis on atonement-based salvation may become wedge issues. Whereas many immigrants are coming from more socially conservative environments in their home countries, young Americans are constantly exposed to more progressive social, scientific, and cultural information. Recent evidence suggests that young adults also are generally more liberal with respect to social issues. This is not a constant, but rather a progressive trend within our focus age group: the younger the person is within the eighteen to forty age range, the more likely they are to be socially liberal and to identify themselves politically with the Democratic party.[11]

Weak Ties, High Mobility

The socially conservative positions of many Evangelical churches cause some young adults initially drawn to the movement ultimately to reject the entire institution of religion. Feeling they cannot identify with the principles of this conservative cross section of the church, they abandon all identification with formal Christian traditions, resulting in a higher number of young people who are religiously unaffiliated.

We see within those young adults who are religiously unaffiliated, not only a contingency who feel neutral or ambivalent about religion overall, but also a considerable percentage who have previously been involved with church, but who walk away from religion as a reaction to some negative experience they have had. This does not exclusively take place within the Evangelical Protestant church, though the more rigid, conservative social environment of many of these churches is diametrically opposed to the social values generally held by the majority of today's younger adults. Our own survey yielded data that would support this claim. Though 81.6 percent of respondents said their first experience with church was positive, 51 percent of our participants answered "yes" when presented with the statement, "I have had a hurtful experience related to church." Of those who have experienced something hurtful in church, 46 percent said that experience now affects their church attendance.

Not all young people walk away from the church. However, the de-emphasized denominational identity fosters a higher degree of mobility among churches and denominations. Young adults tend to be drawn toward places of worship where they feel the greatest connection. This trend generally is driven more by personal relationships than by religious tradition.

In the same *News Hour with Jim Lehrer* piece, Woodruff speaks with Charles Mitchell, a former Catholic who left Catholicism and became a born-again, Evangelical Christian:

> "I was sitting on a plane across the country," says Mitchell, "and I was all of a sudden just really taken up with everything that was waiting for me when I got home. All this stuff that I'd been hearing in this Christian fellowship finally resonated. I have no idea what I said but, 'Dear God, I want a personal relationship with you. Please help me,' or something. That

was it. Got off the plane, told my friends. They all cried. So I was converted."[12]

Though the Evangelical movement draws more young adults, one cannot assume that those who attend Evangelical churches monolithically ascribe to a particular agenda. The Baylor study found that, though one third of all Americans attend an Evangelical Protestant church, only 15 percent use the term *evangelical* to describe their religious identity, and only 2 percent believe it is the best description for their beliefs.[13] Less than one third of the people who attend Evangelical congregations refer to themselves as evangelical. This not only means that more than 67 percent of people in Evangelical churches do not consider themselves to be Evangelicals, but it also means that approximately 15 million Americans who do attend other churches, or who do not attend church at all, identify themselves as evangelical.

Relationship over Religion

Woodruff found that young adults emphasize a personal relationship with God over loyalty to church or dependence on religious rituals or structures. Adora Mora, a first-generation Nigerian-American, notes that, though she attends church every week with her family, it is not as important as her personal connection with God. "I believe in personal relationships with God," she says. "I don't really believe in church. My mom doesn't like me to say that, but it's the truth. I believe my church is sitting in my house, writing a letter to God about what He's done for me, or about good and bad things that have happened with my life and how we'll overcome them together."[14]

Daisy Cooper also echoed this sentiment during the *Lehrer* interview. "I'm not into religion," she explains. "I have a relationship. Religion is…that's what's like…that's what sparks confusion, and God is not the author of confusion. So a religion is what blocks people from getting the real.[15]

We experienced a similar story over Christmas in 2006. Amy met up with an old high school friend, who we'll call Dana. She grew up in a family that had no connection with organized religion, and she only began visiting church when Amy invited her during their junior year in high school. She was baptized the following year but fell away from attending church after leaving for college.

Now in her early thirties, she has sought a source of grounding and greater purpose, both for her life and for her young daughter. She now attends a nondenominational Bible church in her hometown, which she claims has opened her eyes to a new perspective. Though she appreciates the classes, preaching, and music, she insists that the meaning she finds is on a more personal level: "It's not about religion," she said. "It's about relationships."

What We Found

In our own Web-based survey, we gathered the opinions of people between the ages of eighteen and forty about their religious experiences and perspectives on faith. We asked people about their perceptions of church, God, and Christians in separate questions.

Following are the results from several of those questions. Under the "response average" column, the lower the number is, the more affirmative the average response is. For example, a response of "strongly agree" is given a value of 1. An answer of "strongly disagree" is given a value of 5. Answers are averaged to give a quantitative sense of group consensus. We also include the percentage of answers within each category, to give a sense of how broadly distributed the groups opinions were.

Please share your opinions about the following statements: "Churches are...						
	STRONGLY AGREE	SOMEWHAT AGREE	NEUTRAL/ NO OPINION	SOMEWHAT DISAGREE	STRONGLY DISAGREE	RESPONSE AVERAGE
Necessary	27% (158)	25% (147)	14% (79)	8% (48)	26% (149)	2.80
Healthy	12% (71)	33% (194)	18% (104)	20% (116)	17% (99)	2.96
An important part of my life	33% (193)	16% (91)	10% (59)	7% (38)	35% (202)	2.94
Focused on what's important	7% (39)	29% (167)	15% (86)	27% (158)	23% (132)	3.30
Offering valuable programs for me	11% (65)	24% (143)	17% (102)	18% (103)	29% (171)	3.29
Responsible with money	6% (37)	29% (170)	28% (165)	17% (102)	19% (109)	3.13
Comforting places	23% (133)	41% (240)	14% (80)	11% (63)	11% (67)	2.47

Similar to this question, we asked about perception of church:

Please give your opinion of the following statements: "In general churches are..."						
	STRONGLY AGREE	SOMEWHAT AGREE	NEUTRAL/ NO OPINION	SOMEWHAT DISAGREE	STRONGLY DISAGREE	RESPONSE AVERAGE
Safe places	26% (150)	42% (244)	12% (67)	13% (73)	8% (47)	2.35
Growing	18% (107)	32% (186)	21% (120)	24% (138)	5% (28)	2.64
Becoming obsolete	14% (79)	20% (117)	20% (117)	24% (140)	22% (128)	3.21
Geared to people my age	4% (22)	19% (109)	20% (116)	34% (198)	23% (134)	3.54
In need of serious changes	48% (279)	33% (192)	12% (69)	5% (28)	2% (13)	1.80

These results suggest that, though these respondents generally consider churches to be safe places and that they are necessary, they seldom focus on the needs of young adults. Further enforcing this sense that churches are not engaged in the matters most relevant to young adults is that four out of five respondents feel that the church as a whole is in need of serious change.

Following are responses participants offered regarding images they have of themselves:

Offer your opinion of the following statements:						
	STRONGLY AGREE	SOMEWHAT AGREE	NEUTRAL/ NO OPINION	SOMEWHAT DISAGREE	STRONGLY DISAGREE	RESPONSE AVERAGE
I am a spiritual person.	54% (313)	24% (139)	6% (36)	4% (23)	13% (74)	1.98
I am a religious person.	29% (171)	20% (119)	10% (58)	10% (60)	30% (177)	2.92
Church is a necessary part of spiritual life.	27% (158)	20% (115)	5% (32)	12% (68)	36% (211)	3.10
I have a desire to grow spiritually.	60% (352)	19% (109)	5% (30)	4% (24)	12% (69)	1.89
I feel like church has something important to offer me.	30% (175)	24% (138)	5% (31)	12% (68)	30% (173)	2.87

I am aware of the services and programs offered at my local churches.	31% (181)	31% (183)	9% (50)	14% (79)	15% (90)	2.51
Church is an important part of my own spiritual growth.	34% (199)	15% (90)	5% (32)	10% (60)	35% (204)	2.97

Perhaps the most interesting comparison in this set of data is that, while three fourths of all participants identify themselves as spiritual, just less than half claim to be religious. Though nearly 80 percent have a desire to grow spiritually, again just under half believe that church is a necessary part of that spiritual growth process. This, combined with the previous data, suggests not only that a large contingency of young adults consider religion to be out of touch or neglecting the needs of their peer group, but also that even a majority of those who do attend church regularly are not particularly satisfied with the direction of the church, and hence feel like major changes are needed even though they participate.

Some believe that these results imply a trend toward more private, personal spiritual experience over corporate worship. However, our study found that more than three out of four participants are willing to share their spiritual experience with others. Furthermore, nearly 80 percent acknowledged that they would attend a church if it offered the things that were important to them. This large percentage suggests that, although many are discouraged or even disillusioned by their experiences with church, a significant majority of young adults are still open to some type of formal, corporate religious experience.

How young adults express or share this experience is another matter. One cannot assume they view physical church structures as particularly sacred. In our research, 72.3 percent experience God as much or more in nature as they do in church. This does not mean that they only experience God when alone, but perhaps in trying to reach out to a generation so constantly surrounded by a prefabricated, manufactured environment, churches should make a greater effort to go beyond such an institutional setting in order to explore common ground for a shared spiritual experience.

To the central point of this chapter, we should consider how our participants perceive God:

Please give your opinion of the following statements: "God is..."						
	STRONGLY AGREE	SOMEWHAT AGREE	NEUTRAL/ NO OPINION	SOMEWHAT DISAGREE	STRONGLY DISAGREE	RESPONSE AVERAGE
Loving	65% (377)	7% (39)	14% (82)	1% (7)	13% (77)	1.91
Distant	8% (47)	10% (58)	18% (105)	16% (95)	48% (277)	3.85
Judgmental	15% (87)	14% (84)	17% (98)	18% (104)	36% (210)	3.46
Merciful	58% (338)	9% (55)	15% (87)	3% (15)	15% (88)	2.07
All-powerful	47% (273)	13% (77)	17% (97)	7% (39)	17% (97)	2.33
All-knowing	54% (316)	13% (73)	14% (82)	3% (20)	16% (91)	2.14
Present everywhere	64% (376)	8% (49)	12% (70)	2% (11)	13% (77)	1.91

That participants perceive God as primarily loving, ever-present, and merciful is an affirmative trend. It suggests that, on the whole, we are not as cynical, or at least skeptical, about our experience of God as we are about our encounters with church. Less than 20 percent consider God to be distant, and less than 30 percent view God as judgmental, offering an image of God within the young adult community that is inhered with qualities of hope, love, and engagement.

On the other hand, the same group views Christians as a group in a quite different light:

Please give your opinion of the following statements: "Christians are...."						
	STRONGLY AGREE	SOMEWHAT AGREE	NEUTRAL/ NO OPINION	SOMEWHAT DISAGREE	STRONGLY DISAGREE	RESPONSE AVERAGE
Focused on saving souls	10% (57)	36% (207)	24% (137)	20% (115)	10% (55)	2.83
Hypocrites	22% (124)	49% (279)	14% (81)	9% (52)	6% (36)	2.30
Compassionate	16% (90)	48% (272)	17% (95)	13% (76)	6% (37)	2.47
Judgmental	27% (157)	51% (294)	8% (47)	9% (50)	4% (23)	2.10
Open-minded	6% (36)	25% (142)	14% (80)	33% (191)	22% (123)	3.39
Conservative	16% (94)	45% (258)	22% (124)	11% (64)	5% (31)	2.44
Anyone who lives in a Christlike way	7% (97)	30% (169)	20% (115)	16% (89)	18% (102)	2.88
The only ones who will get to heaven	8% (43)	6% (33)	15% (86)	11% (65)	60% (345)	4.11

The most frequent words identified with Christians in this survey were "judgmental" and "hypocrites." Least commonly identified with Christians were the terms "the only ones who will get into heaven" and "open-minded." Clearly, a disconnection exists between people's views of God and those within the Christian faith who claim to be living out the call of God. This difference implies that the issues within church are not simply programmatic dissatisfaction or a general institutional resistance; the perception of Christians overall is that we do not practice what we preach and that we are more consumed with judging others than with connecting with people in a compassionate, open-minded way.

Keep in mind that nearly 60 percent of respondents identify themselves as Christians and that most of the people who did not complete the survey to this point identified themselves as atheist or agnostic. This means that these perceptions are frequently coming from within the Christian faith, and not just from those who don't consider themselves to be Christians.

This confirms that both the church as a whole and Christians as individuals have the burden of proof upon them. Rhetoric and rituals ring hollow if they are not married to an active demonstration of the Christian gospel message in our ministry, our lives, and our relationships. The questions are: How do we begin to engage people in dialogue about their faith? How do we share with others what we believe in a way that is meaningful to them, is not alienating, and respects where they are? A look at the evidence raised in the Baylor study may offer one such opportunity. Their findings about and manner of discussing images of God may provide the dialogic door through which we may all enter together and in the process, learn much about one another's faith experience.

America's Four Gods

With such a high degree of mobility among churches and with ever-weakening ties to particular denominations, church leaders may find it challenging to know who is in the congregation on any given Sunday. Milagro Christian Church, our new church in Pueblo, is a good example. Though we are affiliated with the Christian Church (Disciples of Christ), people who identify themselves as traditionally affiliated with Disciples are in the minority. There are as many people in our church who came from the Roman Catholic tradition as there are lifelong Disciples. This, in part, is due to the heavy influence of Catholicism in the southern Colorado area. It is more the rule than the exception that when church attendees are asked about their religious identity at Milagro, rather than responding, "I am a..." they say, "I was raised 'X,' but now I'm just searching."

We also have an equal number of people who come with no previous church identity or experience. Some consider themselves both Christian and Buddhist, while others come from a more Evangelical tradition. We struggle to develop a common language and point of entry for such a disparate group. While some desire deep spiritual enrichment, others are tentative about even being there. Many from the Roman Catholic tradition call our services "mass" and even call Amy a priest. Some kneel and cross themselves, and others raise their palms to the sky during our worship music time. A few watch everyone else nervously for cues, clearly unfamiliar with the corporate responses, songs, and readings.

Welcome to the new church.

A portion of the Baylor study resonated for us as both a strong predictor for people's existing beliefs and also as a nonthreatening framework for theological discussion among people of all backgrounds and comfort levels. This section of the report is titled "America's Four Gods."

Researchers found that, by determining more about people's perception of God, they could predict much more about their moral and political beliefs than by looking at their faith background.[16] The survey asked twenty-nine questions about participants' understanding of God, and from those responses they developed a formula for determining where their God image fell along a two-dimensional spectrum.[17] The two dimensions include:

- *God's level of engagement:* The extent to which individuals believe that God is directly involved in worldly and personal affairs
- *God's level of anger:* The extent to which individuals believe that God is angered by human sins and tends toward punishing, severe, and wrathful characteristics[18]

From the results they gathered, they developed a graph that identifies four God image types (see graph on page 45).[19]

Obviously, one can understand and relate to God in myriad ways, but by creating four general categories, we can begin to understand one another's theology, moral values, and other important factors

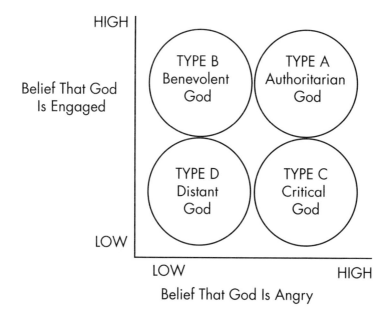

that inform our worldviews. Though four categories are on the chart, people can fall in five areas in their understanding of God:

1. *Type A–Authoritarian God:* God is highly involved in daily life and world affairs. God helps in personal decision making and is responsible for global events (natural, economic, etc.). God is angry and capable of punishing the unfaithful/ungodly.
2. *Type B–Benevolent God:* God is active in daily life, but God is mainly a force of positive influence and is less willing to condemn or punish individuals.
3. *Type C–Critical God:* God really does not interact with the world, but observes and views the current state of things unfavorably. God's displeasure will be felt in another life. Divine justice may not be of this world.
4. *Type D–Distant God:* God is not active in the world and not angry. God is a cosmic force that set the laws of nature in motion, does not "do" things, or hold clear opinions about world events.
5. *Atheists:* Certain that God does not exist, but may still hold strong perspectives concerning morality and social order.[20]

The study extrapolates from the findings to determine the breakdown of God imagery within the greater American population:

- 31.4 percent believe in an Authoritarian God.
- 25 percent believe in a Benevolent God.
- 23 percent believe in a Distant God.
- 16 percent believe in a Critical God.
- 5 percent are atheists.[21]

The data describe many revealing trends that may help us relate better to a diversity of views within and outside our churches. For example, gender and ethnicity are determining factors when considering God image. Women are more than 50 percent more likely to ascribe to an engaged God image (Type A or B), while men are more likely to be drawn toward a distant God concept (C or D), or to be atheists. Though the four God image categories are evenly distributed across the board, a majority of African Americans (52.8 percent) believe in an Authoritarian God. Geographic distribution also plays a part, as Southerners are more prone to view God as Authoritarian, and more Midwesterners see God as Benevolent. Meanwhile, those in the East lean toward a Critical God view, and their Western counterparts see God as more Distant.[22]

God image also says a good deal about people's expected religious practices. Just over half (50.9 percent) of those who believe in an Authoritarian God attend church on a weekly basis, and just under one third of those with a Benevolent God image go to weekly service. However, only one in ten with a Critical image of God goes to church regularly, and the ratio drops to one in twelve for people who believe in a Distant God.

Interestingly, atheists are not the ones most likely to claim never to attend church. People with an image of a Distant God are twice as likely never to attend church (41.5 percent) than atheists (20.2 percent). These trends mirror the results for prayer as well, indicating that people with an engaged concept of God are five to ten times more likely to pray than those who perceive God as disengaged from daily life.[23]

Age is an interesting indicator of likely God images too. People between the ages of 18 and 30 are the most likely to maintain an Authoritarian image of God (40.2 percent), while one third of those aged 31–44 have an Authoritarian view. The percentages drop below 30 percent for all persons over the age of 44. The 18–30 group also is least likely to believe God is Benevolent (13.4 percent), and the 31–44-year-olds are not far behind (20.9 percent). On the other hand, more than one fourth of all people over the age of 44 have a Benevolent view of God. Younger people are also least likely to view God as Critical (average of 14.4 percent for ages 18–44), but are the most likely ones to see God as Distant (average of 25.9 percent for ages 18–44). The tendency toward atheism also grows with each respectively younger age group, so that those between the ages of 18 and 30 are 50 percent more likely to be atheists than those over the age of 65.[24]

God images also say a great deal about what someone is likely to believe about Jesus and about scripture. Most people who see God as Authoritarian are biblical literalists (60.8 percent) and are more than twice as likely to be literalists than are those with a Benevolent (26.5 percent), Critical (10.2 percent), or Distant (2.5 percent) God image.

With respect to people's understanding of Jesus' relationship to God, all of the numbers were surprisingly low. Only four in ten with an Authoritarian God view believe Jesus is the Son of God (41.3 percent), followed by just over one in four with a Benevolent view (27.8 percent), and just over one in seven with a Critical (14.4 percent) and Distant (16.0 percent) understanding of God. Not surprisingly, no one identified as atheist claimed to be a biblical literalist, and none believe Jesus is the Son of God.[25]

Finally, we should consider the differences among denominations. While more than two thirds of those who attend African American Protestant churches (68.0 percent) believe God is Authoritarian, just over half of Evangelical Protestants share this view (52.3 percent), followed by less than one quarter of Mainline Protestants (23.7 percent) and Catholics (22.6 percent). Catholics and Mainline Protestants are the most likely groups to claim a Benevolent God image (28.2 percent and 26.6 percent, respectively), just edging out Evangelicals (23.6 percent), and more than doubling those from the African American Protestant tradition (12.0 percent). Approximately one in five Catholics, African American Protestants, and Mainline Protestants see God as Critical, while less than one in eight Evangelicals share this view. Mainline Protestants lead the way with respect to a Distant God view (29.3 percent), followed closely by Catholics (29.2 percent), and tripling Evangelicals with a similar attitude (10.8 percent). In this survey, no one from the African American Protestant tradition views God as Distant.[26]

Those who are religiously unaffiliated generally have similar images of God as Mainline Protestants, opting for a distant God image (35.7 percent) over a critical (15.7 percent), Benevolent (5.0 percent), or Authoritarian one (2.9 percent). The main difference is that unaffiliated people are forty times more likely to consider themselves atheists as are Mainline Protestants (40.7 percent versus 0.7 percent), and are one fifth as likely to see God as Benevolent (5.0 percent versus 26.6 percent).

Incidentally, the most likely group to identify themselves as atheists, after those who are unaffiliated, are people from the Jewish tradition (8.3 percent), followed by Catholics (1.3 percent), Mainline Protestants (0.7 percent), and Evangelicals (0.5 percent). No one from the African American Protestant tradition claimed to be atheist.[27]

These four categories of God image also say something about people's positions on so-called "moral" issues. Surveyors asked questions about abortion, marital issues (including gay marriage, premarital sex, etc.), and pornography. Interestingly, the greatest opposition in every case came from those with an Authoritarian God image, followed in all categories by those with Benevolent images, then Critical views of God. Those with a Distant understanding of God had the least opposition to such issues.

On average, people who see God as Authoritarian are fifteen times more likely to oppose abortion in all cases as those with a Distant perception of God. They are also more than two and a half times more likely to oppose gay marriage, three times more likely to oppose divorce, five times more prone to reject the use of pornography, nearly eight times as inclined to label premarital sex as immoral, and more than ten times as likely to condemn premarital cohabitation. However, with respect to the death penalty, people with a Distant God image are more than twice as likely to stand in opposition (27.3 percent) as are those with an Authoritarian view (12.1 percent).[28]

Those who feel the urge at this point to scream out "Can't we all just get along?" can find some comfort in these numbers. All categories of God images respond similarly to the necessity to "take care of the sick and needy," with nearly 63 percent of all respondents claiming this is "very important." Though lower overall, all four groups demonstrated similar agreement about "actively seeking social and economic justice" with an average of almost 37 percent considering this "very important."

Now What?

On the basis of this information, we can conclude the following about general trends among American young adults:

- The group is increasingly polarized with respect to their religious affiliation.
- Though more young adults are likely to be involved with an Evangelical church, they are also more likely to be socially liberal than older people and are also more likely to be atheists and/or religiously unaffiliated.
- The two most common God images among young adults are Authoritarian (engaged, angry) and Distant (disengaged, not angry).
- They have less connection with denominations.
- They tend to view their personal relationships with God and with one another as more important than church or organized religion as a whole.

Some churches believe they have found some critical elements that help ensure success with respect to congregational growth. The Hartford Institute for Religion conducted a study in December of 2006 that drew several conclusions about most growing churches:

- They are multiracial.
- Men make up at least 60 percent of regular attendance.
- Worship styles are generally described as "slightly reverent" or "not at all reverent."
- Some form of percussion instruments are used in worship.[29]

Whether or not these are correlative without being directly causative factors in church growth was not explained, but these trends were common among growing churches. With the exception of the male-to-female ratio, one attraction of such a church appears to be that it more closely reflects the culture outside the doors. The question then arises: Is the church intentionally supposed to be set apart or not?

Thomas Bandy warns of the risk of investing too much faith in such relatively superficial components of worship. In a January 2006 wire article released by *The Christian Science Monitor,* he stresses that a particular sort of leader must help "build consensus and trustworthy spiritual authority."[30] Otherwise, such efforts to join these trends will come across as cheap, novel marketing ploys. Also, without a strong foundation and shared vision among church leadership, such changes will add stress and conflict, which can actually lead to lower attendance. In the same article, Bandy warns churches not to measure success entirely based upon attendance numbers, forgoing core identity and values to accommodate a broader audience.

Ultimately, we question whether the healthiest growth can happen at anything but a measured pace, particularly for smaller churches. A relational infrastructure must exist to allow those existing worshipers to genuinely connect with those who come through the door. After all, regardless of worship styles, church architecture, or programmatic amenities, what more young adults are showing us is most important to them is relationship, above all else. A loving relationship upon which a healthy church can grow does not exist in any just-add-water formula for success. It lies in the willing hearts and hands of its faithful to take risks, go out into the community, seek out the needs among the people around them, and act out of love and compassion rather than being driven by an expected outcome.

In a later chapter, titled "God of Rock," we talk about an experience with a large church in Texas, which some might consider to be quite successful. Thousands worship there every week in half a dozen services. The worship bulletins are as slickly produced as any business brochure, and they have comfortable, reclining stadium seating in the sanctuary. Upon entering, worshipers see plasma screens and hear professional-caliber music. The sermons are simple and are illustrated with bullet points, both on the screens and in the bulletins. One simply can come in, experience the service, and leave without ever speaking to anyone. We know, because we did it. The risk in such a worship environment that demands so little of those in attendance is that a sort of complicity develops between the church and its members. As long as people keep coming and keep giving, the church will help them feel good about themselves, assuring them that they are fulfilling their social obligation to be a part of a church.

This is a generalization for illustrative purposes, of course, as plenty of large churches engage people on a deep, meaningful level. The essence, however, as Bandy points out, is in the spiritual foundation and shared vision of those cultivating the growth of the church.

If today's young adults long for authentic community based on meaningful relationships more than they want to be entertained and shuffled out the back door, then the God image concept provides an exciting framework with which to connect with people. In conducting our research for this book, we found no lack of young adults willing to share their views about spirituality, the church, and their personal values and experiences. They have done so both through our online survey, as well as on videotape. They have shared stories of addiction, heartbreak, and other vulnerable parts of their lives. Why? In some cases, they shared only because we did two simple things: we asked, and then we listened.

Often, churches fall into a constant state of "output mode," coordinating services, sermons, concerts, and other programs that they think people will appreciate. They plan outreach programs and mission trips to meet needs they think should be addressed. They talk to people about their church and evangelize about their faith to people who they think need to hear what they have to say. But how often do we ask questions without expectation? How often do we allow people to be critical of our faith or denomination, of our church, or of us without jumping immediately on the defensive? How often are we guessing about what we think people want and need, rather than taking the time, risk, and effort to ask people before acting?

The online survey we conducted was not as easy emotionally as it might seem. We ran the preliminary model by several people, including ministers, family members, and people both inside and outside the church. We took honest criticism willingly, adjusting questions to try to minimize our biases and exclusive language. Still, once we launched the survey and invited people to take part, in only a matter of hours the criticism came rolling in. Some of it was constructive and respectful, and some was acerbic and hateful. In putting ourselves out there as symbols representing the Christian faith in some way, we drew virtual targets on our own foreheads. It was very hard not to react defensively, but we agreed that people should have the opportunity to vent, and that this was part of the price of asking people their opinion: they just might give it to you.

The other risk is yet to be realized. Some will find fault in the data we collected, in the biases within the population it represents, or our general methodology. The reality of doing this sort of work, though, is the same for those truly invested in building a community of faith. There is inherent risk in offering yourself and your heart up to the world. Sometimes you will get hurt. More than once, you will be disappointed. Still we do what we do because we believe it is right, not because we believe it is safe.

Don't be afraid to ask questions of the community around you. Place surveys on your Web site. Put an ad in the local paper. Stop people on the street and ask them five quick questions about what they think the church does right or wrong and could do to help make the world a better place. Better yet, start from the inside and work your way out. If you don't know the stories, experiences, and theology of the people sitting in the chairs next to you every Sunday, what credibility do you have to go out and tell people you have something they need? Conduct a God image survey within your own congregation and use it to guide constructive dialogue about the commonalities and differences within your congregation. Take some time to assess what sort of God image your building conveys. How about the worship music you use? What about the sermons or your outreach programs? What does your signage say about the God you imagine inside? Which of the four Gods do your advertisements, landscaping, programs, outreach, and social events communicate to the world? Do they match the God you intend to share?

As church leaders, we should never expect people to invest time, money, or energy into our causes unless we are first willing to invest time, energy, and, yes, money in them first. This doesn't mean that we open up our bank accounts and wring them dry for the first person who comes along, but it does mean we have to be driven by spirit, mission, and people more than by budget or agenda. If all we're trying to do is draw people in so we can bring them around to our way of thinking, we should not condescend to ask their opinion in the first place. Clearly, their opinion isn't what matters to us. What matters is that the world reflects back to us what we already believe.

The Coffeehouse Myth

For five hundred years, coffee has been a major global commodity, traded across the Asian, South American, and African continents. Coffeehouses first emerged in the Middle East in the early sixteenth century, frequented only by men at the time. They became hubs of social activity, ad hoc epicenters for informal power brokerage, and a forum within which ideas, stories, and more than a few lies were exchanged.

The popularity of the coffeehouse spread west through the seventeenth century, growing firm roots in Austria, France, Italy, and ultimately throughout Great Britain. Coffeehouse culture became the metaphor for the French Enlightenment, led by great thinkers such as Voltaire, Rousseau, and Diderot.[1] In London, Charles II considered the emerging popularity of coffeehouses as a threat to imperial rule. They were seen as "great social levelers,"[2] where people of all backgrounds and classes could convene. This posed a threat to the stranglehold the British aristocracy tried to maintain over power and intellectual capital.

Late in the seventeenth century, London's coffeehouse scene became a center for trading financial information about stocks and other commodities. Eventually, this small group of traders became what is now known as the London Stock Exchange. Coffeehouse trading circles also gave rise to Christie's and Sotheby's, two of the most famous auction houses in the world.[3]

In the United States, coffeehouses became the focus of a countercultural movement, cultivating the emergence of a wave of folk music and, in part, blues and jazz. Churches first adopted the coffeehouse concept in the 1960s, generally in densely populated urban settings. Religious institutions attempted to replicate the popular social atmosphere of traditional coffeehouses, while offering some theological substance in an alternative setting. In general, these models had modest success and generally lasted only a few years at most.[4] This is partly because the coffeehouse began to wane in its appeal later in the 1960s, not long after churches tried to embrace the social trend.

The 1990s witnessed an explosive reemergence of coffeehouse culture, particularly with the viral growth of major retail coffeehouse chains like Starbucks. Comfortable seating, relaxing music, and a casual atmosphere encouraged customers to spend time in the store, which was counter to the surrounding "to-go" culture. Amid a rapidly accelerating pace of life, the modern coffeehouse encouraged people to slow down and reconnect over a universally appealing cup of coffee. Even the dynamic of coffeehouses as hubs of information exchange has resurfaced in recent years with the advent of wireless Internet and with many stores adopting free book and magazine exchange programs.

Once again, churches have latched onto this social phenomenon as an opportunity to reach out and offer their message in a less formal, less "churchy" environment. As before, such efforts are meeting with mixed degrees of success, often struggling to draw interest from members of the general public who do not already have some connection to the church.

Explanations for this lukewarm reception are multiple and highly subjective. One possibility is that part of the appeal of a coffeehouse is the inherent sense of neutral territory. The atmosphere in most coffeehouses is leisurely, casual, and relatively benign. However, churches by nature are far from neutral. Any religious system brings with it a set of values, traditions, and a message they feel is worth sharing with the world. No matter how comfortable a church coffeehouse may seem, people generally are aware they still are in a church.

Another factor now has to do with the simple ubiquity of commercial coffeehouses. As of October 2006, Starbucks had 12,000 stores, with 8,800 of those located in the United States. The state of Washington already has one coffeehouse for every 11,000 people, but the coffee giant is far from content with their current market share. Their long-term plans include opening a total of 40,000 stores worldwide, which would make them bigger than McDonalds.[5]

The idea that a local church can compete in quality and atmosphere with a company that has nearly limitless capital is challenging at best, though opportunities exist within particular niches. We will consider some of these opportunities toward the end of this chapter, but one simple example is the common offering of free wireless Internet by independent coffeehouses. Whereas Starbucks charges for their Wi-Fi connection, many independents have gained an edge by offering the relatively low-cost technology as an amenity for their faithful customers.

Another stumbling block many churches face is the tendency to overprogram. Though some coffeehouses welcome an occasional acoustic musician or monthly poetry reading, churches often insert activity and noise into every crevice of their coffeehouse environment. People can hardly absorb all that comes at them already on a daily basis and for many an hour in the solace of a coffeehouse lounge chair is a much-needed retreat from the clamor. Too often, however, church coffeehouses focus on activities, music, and other distractions that not only can prove overwhelming, but they also prohibit the social discourse which helped make coffeehouses the popular phenomenon they became in the first place.

Finally, the coffeehouse as a model of outreach still builds on a relatively antiquated passive model of connecting with the community. Following World War II, many churches had to do little more than open their doors in a growing part of town to attract a significant congregation. Jack, a friend of ours who is an Episcopal priest, turns eighty years old this year. He recently told us about the dozens of churches he witnessed in the 1950s who were brimming with worshipers, growing ever larger as the young Baby Boomers helped expand the postwar families. Comparing the church atmosphere of his youth to the contemporary religious climate, Jack confesses that if he was a seminary student today, he might choose another profession. Today's church faces an uphill struggle to prove that they live what they claim and that they truly want what is best for their community. Gone are the days when the altruism of religious institutions was taken for granted.

The bulk of this chapter is committed to a set of interviews conducted by Brian Coates, a minister of a church in Plano, Texas. We mailed a videocamera to Brian and asked him to spend some time documenting what he believed was the essence of young adult spirituality. Brian also works part-time at a local Starbucks, partly for the supplementary income and good benefits, and also for the social networking opportunities it provides. During his time as a Starbucks barista, he has befriended several young adults who have come to know him as Brian, a guy who also works at a church, rather than Rev. Coates, senior pastor. Over time, as they have gotten to know him as a multidimensional human being who breathes the same air they do, he has developed a rapport and trust with them. Though he is a minister, and though none of them is involved in any church activity, they consider him a friend.

Instead of telling his own faith story, Brian decided to ask these four young adults about their experience with church and about the role of faith in today's world. Their responses were personal, sometimes surprising, and generally straight to the point. For the purposes of this book, we'll call the four young people Anna, Sienna, Brad, and Dante. All of them are in their twenties and have some past experience with organized religion, particularly Christianity, and none of them currently attends a church.

The Starbucks Session

Anna enjoyed church as a child, especially the time together with her family. However, an underlying tone of judgment alienated her over time. "They would preach to you, like, 'you have to do this, you have to do that,'" says Anna. "'If you're going to believe, you have to believe this way,' and I'm not all about that."

When asked about her understanding of God, Anna is vague. "The only thing I know about God is that when people die they go to this place," she says. "My family always believed that when we die, we go to this resting place, and you go with the rest of your family with God. I don't know what to think."

Like many people not connected with a consistent religious discipline, Anna generally only seeks God in times of tragedy or crisis. "I think the one time that I actually got hit by it was when my grandmother was dying of cancer," she recalls. "She was in so much pain, and for some reason, I went home and I cried. I was so mad because people say that there's this God and he's supposed to help." She remembers yelling at God out loud, confused by the suffering her grandmother had to endure. Finally, she pleaded for her pain to end. The next day, she says, her grandmother was dead. From that day on, Anna held a deep ambivalence about her understanding of a God who would allow such things to happen.

Brad has a mop of sandy brown hair hanging over his eyes. He looks down at his lap often as he speaks, yet he offers a sort of candor that is rather unexpected based upon his withdrawn appearance. He describes himself as a fanatic for BMX bikes and girls, but hedges when asked about any greater trajectory for his future. Brad's early years in church did not interest him, though he did find a positive social outlet through participation in extreme sports.

"That helped me stay away from drugs and alcohol," he says. "Then I got hurt, and that whole time I would always pray because I thought I was actually a good person back then." A doctor diagnosed him with a torn ligament in his knee, which kept him from participating in skating and biking competitions. After that, Brad fell into a regular pattern of alcohol and drug abuse.

"I started smoking cigarettes just out of boredom," says Brad. "I lost my path. I kind of lost the faith there for a little while, but I'm trying to regain it."

Brad says he wants to believe in God, although he is unsure if he does. "It's scary to think that you're just alone," he says. "Nobody wants to die, and as soon as your brain shuts down, that's just it–all the memories and everything–just gone."

The main resistance Brad has to becoming involved again with a church is a lingering sense that he has missed out on too much during his years outside of church to feel a part of such a closely knit group. Also, he struggles with many of the stories in scripture describing supernatural events and feels uncomfortable with the idea of being forced to believe in something he considers counterintuitive. "So many Bible stories are so far-fetched," says Brad. "Getting swallowed by a whale and living in there for days, that's just kind of far-fetched, I've never been talking to a bush that was on fire."

Though Sienna currently is in school, she too feels a lack of direction in her life. She remembers falling asleep every week during Catholic mass. She attended confirmation classes during her teenage years, but felt no connection to what she took from them. Her parents did not pressure her or her siblings to continue with regular church attendance, so eventually she quit going.

She finds the various rituals of the different religions distancing and even "creepy." She once lost interest in a romantic relationship after her boyfriend tried to coerce her into joining his church.

"I believe in God, just because I've been raised that way," says Sienna. Like Brad, she considers the concept of the absence of God frightening, but her experiences with organized religion have not offered her any distinct concepts of divinity to which she can relate. Like the others in the group, she sees little connection between her own personal understanding of God and the teachings and rhetoric of the church.

Dante, an architecture student, is the most quiet, thoughtful member of the group. He describes himself as content, and he offered the most eclectic personal religious history.

"I remember as a kid, we did go to church every Sunday," he says. "It was a really small town church, really evangelical. We would just go through the motions and block it out and not really listen because we were little kids. Our family stopped going by the time we hit high school. We just blocked religion out of our life for a long time, and I just didn't think about it until I started getting into college and taking philosophy classes."

Dante rekindled an interest in theological matters during some comparative religion courses in college where he cultivated his interest in the philosophical dimensions of world religions, particularly those from the Far East. He read a copy of the Bhagavad Gita that a monk on his college campus shared with him, and he began attending Yoga classes. Dante also was open to more traditional church experiences with a friend of his, though he did not particularly resonate with the teaching. "I just like to keep an open mind," he explains.

Dante says that, although he believes in some greater divine presence, he finds the traditional Christian portrayals of God difficult to reconcile with his own understanding. He perceives life as having some greater mystical purpose and believes the universe is more than a series of cosmic coincidences. However, he is still unclear about what is at the essence of creation. "I feel like there really is something bigger and more important," he says. "I just don't feel like I really know what it is, or who it is."

When asked about their understanding of prayer, the group shared common sentiments. "Praying is a personal thing," says Anna, "and I don't feel very comfortable praying in public. I think you do that in your own time, in your own space. That's part of church that I hate–praying with all these people. And, half the time you don't even know what you're praying about."

Brad acknowledges praying, but generally only in a state of desperation. "I just pray when it's, like, the absolute low point," he says. "I used to pray all the time, but it would be all the same stuff, like, 'Dear God, please watch over my family and friends.' Now I'm so lost it's not even funny. I pray sometimes. I mean, if the reason everything's so crappy right now is because I'm not praying, then I'll start praying, or do something else that makes me not be such a bad person."

Sienna echoed that her prayer life was also waning. Whereas she used to pray all of the time, she now only prays in times of particular need, like when she travels by plane or is facing a particularly challenging test at school. Much like the rest of the group, Dante only admits to praying when a loved one is sick or when he experiences a near miss in his car. Otherwise he, like the others, does not consider prayer to be a regular part of his personal life.

In general, all four young adults perceive God as a scorekeeper or divine disciplinarian, tracking their missteps more than providing wisdom or guidance. Anna asks herself on occasion if she believes God would approve of particular behaviors in which she engages, but otherwise God has little influence over her daily life and choices.

Brad claims to think about God "all the time." But he imagines God being more disappointed with him than anything else. "For the most part, I'm a good person," he says, "and I love all my friends and family. I'd do anything for them." He feels, though, that his sexual impulses particularly place distance between him and the teachings of the churches of his childhood.

"I thought that God was supposed to love you," says Brad. "But I think that a lot of churches come off like, 'God loves you, but he'll cast you into a ring of fire if you don't get baptized.' My friend was saying you can live a perfect life of no sin, but if you don't believe Jesus is the Son of God then you go to hell."

Dante believes that people have two different perspectives about religion. On the one hand, "you're supposed to take morals and values from religion, learn lessons from it, and put those into your life. Like, 'let he who is without sin cast the first stone,' that type thing.

"But then, there's the other side where people think, 'Well, you're not supposed to do something because Jesus is watching. He'll punish you immediately. So, they do it more out of fear and out of feeling like they're obeying, or like they're afraid of doing something against the rules, not so much because they understand that it's wrong. It's more like they're going to be punished and they're trying to save themselves. So, those people sin all week and when Sunday rolls around they'll go to church and feel like they're forgiven for all of it automatically. They have a backwards mentality about the whole point of religion."

Dante also rejects the idea that someone must be baptized in order to join in communion with God after death. He also feels that religious people often inappropriately try to convey a false sense of piety, setting themselves somehow above the fray. "People screw up," he says. The idea, then, is not to be perfect, but to take basic moral lessons from scripture and organized religion, helping to serve as a means to a more God-centered life.

When asked about God's place in the world here and now, the four offered relatively cynical perspectives. Anna, Brad, and Dante focused on the church's claims upon salvation and the religious perception that life principally is a test for passage to heaven after death.

"You hear about all you people that were 'saved,'" says Anna. "I honestly don't know what that means. I have one friend in particular who gets into all this trouble. She basically runs with the trends of all the friends she hangs out with. She says she's saved, but she does all these things. Then she gets so mad at you if you say God's name in vain.

"If people believe in God, then they're viewed as persons who do not do anything bad. But really, people do all kinds of bad things. They just don't say anything about them. That's where I get confused. What are you doing? Why can't you just be truthful?"

Brad says, "Can a thirty-year-old guy can get away with having premarital sex with a fourteen-year-old girl and still get into heaven? Or can someone rape someone else and still go to heaven, or can someone murder someone else and still go to heaven? If they believe Jesus is the Son of God and ask for forgiveness, and still go to heaven, then, that's messed up. Then someone who's never done anything bad, but never got around to getting baptized or doesn't believe, they don't get into heaven, that doesn't make a lot a sense to me. If you believe that Jesus is the Son of God and you've been baptized, then you get into heaven no matter what, right? But if you're just a little humble science professor who sits there all day and hasn't hurt anyone their whole lives, and then they go to hell, that doesn't make much sense to me."

Dante is a proponent of the concept that actions speak louder than words. "If you're generally a person who goes about your day-to-day activities not hurting anybody," he says, "then I think God can be reasonable and let you in even if you didn't go to church. Too many people think that they can do whatever they want, then go get it wiped clean at the end of the week when they go to church on Sunday. That, to me, just seems completely backwards.

"At the same time, if somebody went their whole life and they didn't really try to understand religion, I don't think God would be upset at them for not understanding religion, because it's a lot to try to understand."

Overall, when asked what kind of church would appeal to them, these young adults value authenticity and meaningful relationships over particular worship styles or music selection.

"If you bring new people to the church," says Anna, "don't freak all those new people out and ask them all really personal questions. Be really accepting and open to the people that are coming, and don't have just one way of thinking about things. Get involved with them religiously, but also on a personal level, a friendship level, where you can just talk with them and not have to relate anything to God. We're here to help each other. And, I think that is what church is about."

Brad tends to believe that the initial friendly reception he experiences when meeting church people is little more than a thin veneer. "Stop making fun of my hair," he says, "and stop giving hearty handshakes. Do anything in your possible power to make church less boring. It's so boring, it's not even funny. It hurts your brain. It's like going to school. You don't want to go. Don't make it boring, and don't make it cheesy. Don't only talk about going to hell. Don't try to scare people into being religious. Don't make it seem like you're leading the church just so you won't go to hell.

"I think a lot of people say, 'We're going to make a cool, trendy church, and their idea of that is, 'We're gonna get a guy that's about twenty-six. He's going to come in with the cool, spiky hair that looks like a Backstreet Boy, and he's going to get a guitar out and sing. And all the girls will say, 'He's so cute, I want to do whatever he says.'

"People get the idea that if they play some more trendy or cool songs, it'll be easy to grow a church. But for a guy who's just trying to get into religion, they don't want to go in there and have to sing along to DC Talk and then have to get up and be embarrassed."

Sienna resonates with the discomfort of trying to sing along with music she doesn't know. "Don't have sing-alongs. That is the most ridiculous thing ever. I think if you could sit down with a group of people—something small—and have a conversation once a week, or whenever you wanted to, that's what I would be into. Not, 'Let's all sit here in pews and kneel and pray and sing along.'"

Sienna also advocates for more comparative religious study, examining common mythical and moral themes among the world's religions, rather than touting the superiority of one particular way of thinking. "I can't devote myself a hundred percent to the Catholic Church," she says, "because I believe in other things as well."

Dante recalls going to churches with contemporary praise bands and video screens. He considers this worship style "corny," equating the atmosphere to that of an after-school television special. Also, he struggles with the mythical stories at the center of some religious teaching, particularly when they are presented as literal, absolute truth.

"One of the things that I can't really ever wrap my head around about religion is some of the really far-fetched stories," says Dante, "like flooding the earth and burning bushes, and voices from the sky, and stuff that would be pretty much impossible to believe for a practical person who believes in science. I'm thinking, 'That's impossible. I already don't want to listen to this.'

"But, if they were saying, 'This is what the story says. What kind of lesson can we get out of it?' I think I would be interested. The Bible is not necessarily...carved in stone. Just think of it as guidelines for lessons, morals, and values that we can apply to our real lives.

"There are universal truths to every religion. So, it'd be interesting to go and listen to hear all of the universal claims in all religions. There's a lot of people on earth and a small percentage of them are Christian, so some churches would say, 'The rest of them are wrong.' Are you saying everybody is condemned except for Christians? That's a selfish way of thinking of it. It would be more interesting to talk about the differences."

Common to all four young adults was a sense of estrangement from the traditions and vernacular of organized religion. They share a lack of a religious foundation on which to build a deeply personal—and at the same time an intimately collective—spiritual experience. They find the culture of the church foreign, while also feeling that the barrier between themselves and religion becomes increasingly impenetrable the longer they are uninvolved.

To the degree that we Christians put energy into setting the church apart, these four young adults suggest we are doing more harm than good if our principal goal is to reach beyond those whom we already serve. While the songs, readings, and other practices of our congregations may lend us a sense of security and even a greater communion with God, we may unconsciously be driving wedges between ourselves and the rest of the world.

Though the rituals of worship are essential to the Christian experience, those of us on the inside can easily lose sight of the alien nature of our beliefs and routines to others. On the other hand, our unfettered zeal to share the gospel message of hope and love can come across as opportunistic or even predatory if we are not first invested in the interests and needs of others. We must, then, strike a healthy balance between holding close those things that give our faith its sense of the sacred, while also being willing to meet others where they are, not on our own terms, but in a way that is authentically human first. We earn the right to engage them as Christians once we have earned their trust.

Further, we must be able to address the "so what?" factor. With so much demanding our time, attention, and energy, why bother with church? What difference does it make for us personally, as well as for the greater community or for the world as a whole? If we cannot articulate clearly and simply why the faith we claim is worth the effort, those who are unchurched have no reason to buy what we are selling, so to speak. If we can't sit down over a cup of coffee and explain our own transforming faith story in a way that relates meaningfully to the person next to us, what right do we have to engage in evangelism? If we don't practice what we preach, why should anyone bother to listen? Until the world around us is noticeably different for the better because of our faith, the claim that our religion is little more than hollow rhetoric and duplicity is not only warranted, it is a charge that all Christians must work sincerely to overcome.

Jesus and Java

Molly is a "new church planter" in Elk Grove, California, which means she's trying to start a new church with the support of the Christian Church (Disciples of Christ). The Disciples denomination has set forth an aggressive goal of starting 1,000 new churches by the year 2020. The slogan driving this movement is, "A thousand churches, a thousand ways." Molly's new faith community, the Table of Grace Christian Church, is one example of how churches can embrace the "coffeehouse spirit."

Following is the church's mission statement from their Web site:

> Table of Grace Christian Church seeks to be a haven from the chaos of the world where all sorts of families can explore their Christian spirituality and grow in their faith in a way that is in harmony with their postmodern and intellectually engaged worldview.[6]

The site also acknowledges that an increasing number of people do not feel like the church has anything to offer them, and hence they identify themselves as "spiritual but not religious." The emphasis of Table of Grace's literature is on building relationships, mutual respect, and a balance of challenging not only the spirit but the mind and heart as well. The congregation only comes together for worship once a month, focusing the rest of the time on small group development. When they do meet for worship, the setting is Molly's home.

All of this communicates a number of things to a person considering her faith community. First, they do not discuss membership, statements of faith, or what one must do in order to be saved. The congregation acknowledges that many have been hurt or disaffected by organized religion and that it's acceptable to consider yourself not religious. Further, community is put first, suggesting that the strength of interpersonal trust and mutual enrichment must develop before corporate worship can be emphasized. Molly also emphasizes the need for retreat from the world's chaos. One can infer that, by participating in a Table of Grace event, the atmosphere will be intimate, inviting, and focused on renewal and spiritual growth.

Finally, they focus instead on the intense desire for belonging that everyone shares, particularly young people. Membership inherently implies exclusivity and, to some degree, the need for conformity. At Table of Grace, anyone who shows up belongs. Belonging is more important than membership or a false sense of security or piety.

The emphasis on quiet renewal, interpersonal intimacy, and acceptance of people wherever they are in life reflects the most appealing dynamics of a coffeehouse. By moving monthly events to different homes and other locations, the focus becomes the people involved, rather than the space itself. People take turns hosting book groups and social events, and some activities are held outdoors.

Once a month, the group meets at a local coffeehouse for their church's knitting group. The small team of knitters gets together and knits prayer shawls for people who have requested them or for people in the community who might appreciate the gesture, such as homebound seniors. As the group knits, they talk about their lives and the future of the church, and they share requests for prayer with one another. An incidental, but hardly accidental, advantage of meeting in such a public area is that it opens up many opportunities for discussion with people visiting the coffeehouse. Frequently, someone who enjoys knitting will approach them and ask about their project, and, of course, Molly is happy to share a card with the individual and to invite the person to join them.

A church in Kerrville, Texas, has a unique take on the church coffeehouse model. In addition to providing a quiet environment where adults can relax and socialize, they have included an indoor play area, much like those found at many fast food restaurants, to allow parents a place to bring their children. The combined coffeehouse and play center has begun to draw many parents during the day who stay home with their children, along with families in the evening. Information about church programs is available for those who are interested, but parents also are welcome to read, work on their computers, or chat with others while their children play safely nearby.

In this way, the church offers a unique service not available in traditional coffeehouses. As the parents of a three-year-old boy, we recognize that taking a young child to a regular coffeehouse is anything but relaxing in most cases. The atmosphere is appealing to parents who might not otherwise feel like they have an opportunity to get out of the house and socialize. Immediately, people form a positive association with the church, which has offered this as a service to the community without condition.

Audrey and Kauley Jones recently moved to southern Colorado from Florida intent on starting a Christian ministry in the small town of Walsenburg. Walsenburg did not have a large demand for a new church to immediately support their family, and the last thing the town seemed to need was another traditional church. The Joneses recognized that the youth and young adults of the community had no place to hang out, other than on the streets. Instead of building a church, they started a coffeehouse. Audrey and Kauley both work every day in the coffeehouse and have started to get to know the locals. As they build rapport with customers, someone will ask why they came to town. They explain their vision for ministry, and if the person shows interest, they invite them back for a Bible study, book discussion, or other small group activity held in the back of the store.

Their ministry has no vestments, no piano, bulletins, or pews. Little about the space suggests the faith-based bent, other than quiet Christian music playing in the background and a few religious texts on the shelves. Many who visit the shop simply enjoy their coffee and time with friends and nothing more. If the issue arises, however, they speak openly about their faith and try to engage people about what they feel they need in a faith community. The groups are small, casual, and have no formal lesson plans in most cases. For now, the couple is focused on building a viable business that will allow them to continue engaging in ministry and, along the way, developing trust and interest with the people who come through the doors. Some might not call it a church, but no one can deny it is a real ministry.

"People have a real hunger for God, but they might not feel comfortable in church,"[7] says Kauley about the alternative setting. On Friday evenings, the couple provides free pizza for local teens, and they have already started an expansion in the back that would provide space for a pool table and foosball. They plan to add a Bible study and a twelve-step meeting called Overcomers in the near future. Kauley is even considering offering a hip-hop dance class.

"There are so many wounded people in the world," says Kauley. "We just want to be here for them."[8]

Habit, Tradition, and Ritual

Christmas is a hectic time for many. For those who lead a church, the season can bring a combination of anticipation, dread, and an insatiable sense of urgency. This high religious holiday carries so many expectations that can never be met, and the challenge of remaining focused on the "true meaning of Christmas" always seems somewhat elusive. No matter how firmly we resolve not to buy into the superficial trappings of the holidays, the ubiquity of various messages all around us grows every year, subsuming other holidays along the way.

At one time it was improper to decorate for Christmas before Thanksgiving. Now there are hints of the coming holiday by Halloween or earlier. Memorial Day may not be far behind. With a protracted Christmas season come ever-growing anticipation and less realistic expectations of what is to come. By the time the long-awaited day arrives, the songs and images that announced its coming merge into an annoying cacophony of white noise, losing much of their aesthetic and symbolic preciousness. When Christmas finally comes, people almost always experience some sense of letdown, as the buildup outshines the day itself.

Our family waited until the weekend following Thanksgiving to adorn the living room with our fake tree, stockings, and a half dozen or so nativity sets. Our son, Mattias, who is three, could hardly wait for the day itself, always frustrated with the answer he received several times a day when he would ask, "It is Christmas yet?" We caught him undecorating the tree several times, and he found and unwrapped one early gift from his aunt.

As we are in ministry, we like to think our child looks at Christmas differently. We told him the story of Jesus' birth a number of times, but when we ask him what Christmas is about, he happily says, "Santa!"

Before Christmas existed, a celebration known as Saturnalia took place from December 17 to 25. The seventeenth was the recognized birthday of the god Saturn, and the twenty-fifth marked the birth of Sol Invictus (the undefeated sun), the god celebrated for reclaiming daylight after the winter solstice. The festivities included an exchange of gifts, along with much drinking, gambling, and carousing. While rejecting the debauchery, Christians held on to the tradition of gift exchange, making it part of the new Christmas tradition.

Another Persian religion known as Mithraism also jumped into the mix. It claimed the twenty-fifth as the birthday of their god, Mithra, who was identified closely with Sol Invictus of the Greek tradition. Although Christians were third on the bandwagon, the spread of Christianity through the Roman Empire in the third and fourth centuries C.E. gave it a strong foothold.

Not everyone was fond of the idea of celebrating Jesus' birth with feasts and gifts. Origen, one of Christianity's earliest leaders, denounced the practice as contrary to Christian principles. However, Constantine saw an opportunity to reconcile varying views of Jesus with an official holiday. Christmas became an official Roman holiday in 350 C.E., helping to assert the position that Christ was divine from birth, not just following his baptism.

It would be another thousand years, however, until Christmas became a holiday synonymous with large-scale celebration. King Richard II put on elaborate feasts, reminiscent of the festivals Christmas had originally recreated in its own image. In the seventeenth century, Christmas was all but outlawed, condemned by Puritanical powers as hedonism behind a thin veil of piety.

Many early Americans also looked sourly upon Christmas as part of the Anglican tradition they left behind. By the nineteenth century, it became the stuff of romantic nostalgia, depicted by Charles Dickens and other scribes as a time for family, sharing, and celebration. Soon retailers saw an opportunity, and the rest is history.

One can easily get disenchanted about such a sacred day being consumed by consumption. But it helps to know that modern merchants aren't the first to mold December 25 into something other than what it first was. Just as our religious predecessors struggled to co-opt the traditions of other cultures, infusing them with sacred Christian significance, so are we now engaged in a similar effort to maintain what we believe is the most important message of Christmas. Secular traditions and the frenzy of consumerism are a tough match for a simple story about a child born in poverty two thousand years ago. The nativity story suffers from abstraction, while the world around us offers immediate fulfillment.

As told in the chapter titled "The Coffeehouse Myth," some young adults view church and the Bible as conglomerations of fairy tales and myths that have no connection to their present experience. While they all have at least a cursory knowledge of some Bible stories, none of them shares an experience of a thoughtful, rich theological experience. A few of them find more applicable and intellectually challenging content in their exploration of Eastern religion and philosophy, suggesting they generally seek some greater relevance. However, their general perceptions of Christianity are effectively caricatures, with one young woman likening her understanding of scripture to the myths she has been told about Santa Claus.

Tamara Draught, author of *Strapped: Why America's 20- and 30-Somethings Can't Get Ahead*, argues that today's young adults are more family oriented than their parents, placing family before career and material acquisition in many cases.[1] However, a perfect financial storm of sorts has descended on this cross section of the culture that has burdened them with historically unprecedented debt loads. While tuition subsidies have shrunk in recent decades in proportion to escalating college expenses, more entry-level jobs are now part-time than ever before. More young people are working multiple jobs with no benefits, while also burdened with a crippling combination of credit card and student loan debt. As a result, many college graduates are moving back in with their parents.

The *Akron Beacon Journal* offers some sobering statistics about debt load trends among young adults:

- The average credit debt among young adults ages twenty-five to thirty-four increased 55 percent between 1992 and 2001 to $4,088 a month.
- The average indebted household in that age group now spends almost a quarter of every dollar earned on debt payments.

- Among the two thirds of those young adult households with incomes below $50,000, nearly one in five with credit card debt is in debt hardship, spending more than 40 percent of their income on debt, including mortgages and student loans.
- Credit card debt among the youngest adults (those ages eighteen to twenty-four) skyrocketed 104 percent between 1992 and 2001 to $2,985 per month.[2]

These statistics alone are enough to help us understand the bleak attitude of many young adults about their future. While they carry more debt than any other generation before them, they also stand to be the first generation not to exceed previous generations in income potential. Financial issues are only one concern. Matters of sexuality and substance abuse continue to grow in their impact on young adult culture, not to mention issues of body image. In two churches where we have worked directly with the youth, a majority of the young women already had struggled in the past or currently were dealing with an eating disorder. In one particular church, every female in the youth group had experienced difficulty with an eating disorder.

If we inherit the faith of our parents, our model is one of church on Sunday, followed by a life conducted in pursuit of consumption, career, expended resources, fragile ecosystems, broken homes, and political, corporate, and religious mistrust. All the while, we are not taught that the most important thing in life is to grow to fulfill God's call of service to the world, but rather to be the best, to get the best education, and to land the best career with the largest salary and greatest prestige.

We're left with many lingering questions: Why bother? To what end is this life in pursuit of earthly success? What more is there? The dichotomy between what is taught from the pulpit and what has been modeled for us outside the church emasculates the gospel message with respect to practical application. After all, why take advice from a hypocrite?

Meanwhile, the critical issues with which youth and young adults are contending on a daily basis, such as those mentioned above, go unaddressed by the church in most cases. With respect to fiscal responsibility, sexuality, drugs, alcohol, and other matters of healthy self-care, religion is either perilously silent or monolithically prohibitive: "It's all bad. Just don't do it, period." Rather than intentionally fostering our young people through a process of responsible discernment, we preach at them about what not to do, then we wonder why the messages they receive during Sunday school and worship ring hollow. To paraphrase one young man from our "Starbucks Session" interview, it's hard to understand how an isolated story about a burning bush can help us be better people.

What do we do, then, to overcome the sense of removal we often have with such stories from scripture? Are the acts of worship during Christmas and throughout the year truly sacred rituals, or have they become inflexible traditions, or even empty habits? In this chapter, we consider the differences among habits, traditions, and rituals, as well as how we might help connect people with the greater meaning they seek in a corporate faith experience. We look at some unique traits of today's young adult culture within the paradigm of the human imagination and how sacred ritual can help fill in the spaces that many of us experience without a meaningful connection to God.

Habit

Habits say something about what lies beneath the surface of observable human behavior. Generally not conscious, habits manifest themselves in repeated actions, often in particular settings. Sometimes, we are not even aware when we are acting habitually. Even if we are aware, we may feel we have little power to change our behavior. Habit can be described as "the unself-conscious background of self-conscious experience."[3] Though we may realize we are acting habitually, we may not be fully conscious of the driving forces behind those actions. These compulsions can tell us something about our unconscious views of ourselves and understanding of the world, however.

David Morris, associate professor of philosophy at Trent University, claims that habit "mediates between unconscious nature and self-conscious spiritual life."[4] In this way, habits express something generally inexpressible about our unconscious nature. The self-conscious spiritual life of which Morris speaks is an idealized vision of what we long to be. With this understanding, our habits may bridge the gap between what we want to become and those parts of our most primal self that we hardly understand. Raised to the proper level of consciousness, we can learn deeply about ourselves through acknowledgment of and dialogue about our individual and corporate habits. Unmitigated, habits are a downward spiral, leading to the consuming mire of addiction:

> One tries to live one's life well, one tries to head toward one's own future, yet one's life unfolds from habits that seemingly "run" one from one's past–past life implies itself in the fabric of the present and thus extrudes a shell around one's future. In the case of an unshakable habit, an addiction, habit is no mere shell: it is a prison. The matter of this shell or prison, which flares into prominence in the attempt to live well, is time.[5]

Taken to the degree of addiction, habits go from being defining, though somewhat limiting, traits of our nature to becoming the essence of our existence. Their role in our lives grows, consuming all else, including the "self-conscious spiritual life" toward which we are otherwise directed. The nature of habits, if they grow into addictions, is to focus increasingly inward, fixating of the amelioration of pain and the avoidance of suffering. We become more isolated, losing hope and a vision for a future other than our present state, thus feeding on a cyclical pattern of self-destructiveness and guilt.

Entertainment, or distraction, and addiction, for Morris, are a "pervasive and inherent background of secular life." The solution for emerging from this addictive cycle "seems to be through what amounts to religious community."[6] This community includes not only church but also twelve-step support groups like Alcoholics Anonymous. Within a nurturing faith community we find the necessary tools to overcome absorption with self, redirecting ourselves toward a self-conscious spiritual life.

In being a nurturing community that leads to healing, the church has a great opportunity to live out its gospel mission to help mend the world's brokenness. Unfortunately, the church environment also provides a unique platform for addicts and predators alike to act on their darkest impulses under the guise of church leadership.

Pastorates often present a particular combination of power, implicit trust, and a lack of checks and balances that can allow unrecognized destructive habits to cause tremendous damage. One only has to look at the troubles within the Roman Catholic Church in recent years or at fallen leaders such as Ted Haggard for a systemic example of gross misconduct under the protective cloak of religion. As noted in another chapter, nearly half of the respondents to our own online survey claim to have had a hurtful experience related to church. Half of those say that the experience has affected their attendance at church.

If Morris's claim that habits indicate the unconscious dimensions of our nature, then people would present behavioral indicators of potentially damaging behavior before they got out of control. However, recognizing these dangerous habits within congregations is only one step: we also must hold one another accountable for our actions, raising the standard of conduct to the necessary level to earn the trust that has been damaged by so many acts of betrayal. Somewhere along the way, some Christians adopted the mistaken impression that, in order to be a good and faithful servant of the gospel, one must always be nice. We believe we should avoid hurting others' feelings at all costs. If you don't have something nice to say, don't say anything at all.

God calls Christians to speak the truth in love, to recognize both the divine spirit and the hurting child in everyone, and to take action to evoke the strength for healing that we require in order to realize God's grace in our lives and churches. Ignoring unhealthy habits within our midst makes us enablers of the problem. By taking no action to mediate a solution, we are complicit in the pain caused by the addictive behavior.

Tradition

Traditions are integral to church identity. Past stories and present experiences converge in a meaningful intersection of timeless significance. There is a transcendent nature about long-held traditions, and Christians can find great value in employing them as a vehicle by which we pass along stories to future generations. A risk is involved, however, in relying on the permanence and comfort of tradition, offering a sense of false certitude or righteousness. Terry Eagleton, professor of cultural theory and John Rylands Fellow at Manchester University, offers the following words of warning about the power of tradition:

> An appeal to cultural tradition simply means that doing something for a very long time is the next best thing to being right. The reason why you go in for honor killings or racial lynchings is because this is the kind of thing you go in for. The word "culture", like the words "taste" or "evil", means

among other things: don't argue. What we do is what we do. We cannot justify it rationally, but neither can you justify your objections to it. So we might as well declare a truce. As long as you let us get on with female infanticide, which is completely unremarkable in our society, we shall let you get on with the domestic violence that figures so richly in your own cultural tradition. Cultural relativism of this sort is highly convenient for the ruling powers.[7]

The danger of cultural relativism lies within every tradition that is conducted without regard for the possible negative consequences it has on others. An example of this might be the use of the confederate flag in certain Southern cultural circles. While some argue it is a symbol of cultural heritage, for many it cannot be separated from the oppression of slavery. Therefore, in choosing to maintain the tradition of certain symbols of the confederacy, people implicitly value their need for tradition over the harm or division it may cause.

The greatest risk of damaging traditions going unmonitored is in a homogenous, insulated community. While some churches are making great efforts to become more pluralistic and reflective of the community around them, many others are content to maintain a status quo relationship with respect to their valued traditions.

Rev. Dr. Martin Luther King Jr. addressed this very issue in his well-known speech at Western Michigan University in 1963:

We must face the fact that in America, the church is still the most segregated major institution in America. At 11:00 on Sunday morning when we stand and sing and Christ has no east or west, we stand at the most segregated hour in this nation. This is tragic. Nobody of honesty can overlook this. Now, I'm sure that if the church had taken a stronger stand all along, we wouldn't have many of the problems that we have. The first way that the church can repent, the first way that it can move out into the arena of social reform is to remove the yoke of segregation from its own body.[8]

It is appealing to imagine we have responded fully to this call in the subsequent decades since this speech, but in reality, our churches remain largely homogenous. We cannot simply say that we welcome everyone: We must go out of our way to remove the yoke of which Dr. King speaks. Our traditions, though perhaps not explicitly exclusive to one particular group, create an atmosphere of internality. Without intending to, everything from the songs we sing to the prayers we speak and the symbols we hang on our walls can whisper, ever so subtly, "You are not welcome here."

Our call is not to become a color-blind, class-blind church. The idea is not to eradicate all differences, creating a melting pot of religious culture within which we can discern no distinctions. First, we must recognize that "if our being cultural animals is a source of division, it is also what we have universally in common," says Eagleton. "Besides, to say that we are all cultural animals is to say that we are all needy and vulnerable... It is on this shared vulnerability, not on cultural differences, that any decent politics must surely be built."[9]

Christians will face vulnerability in opening ourselves up to the world, in exposing the best and worst of what church has to offer, and in offering our gifts to a people longing for hope. Welcoming people different from ourselves is only one step. We must first examine our traditions and consider the purpose, history, and spiritual necessity of those practices to which we cling. In fostering a desire to reflect the greater society with respect to age, ethnicity, gender, and socioeconomic status, we must accept as a foregone conclusion that our church will change. We cannot pick and choose which traditions we protect and which we challenge. In making ourselves vulnerable, we also commit to examining our habits and traditions, placing them under a critical and objective lens.

Of course, not all traditions are inherently divisive or negative. However, we all too easily fall into a place of comfort with our ways, while unaware of what this communicates to everyone else. It is not a difficult leap to begin sanctifying traditions as holy or inviolate, with no logical or spiritual basis. In creating a sanctuary around ourselves within the church, we build walls that keep all forces who would challenge that sanctity at arm's length. The responsibility is on us to ask ourselves as communities of faith: Would we give up all that we have and all that we are in the spirit of Christ, if God called us to do so?

Jesus challenges us to set free our viselike grip on our very lives in order to realize true life as God intends (Mt. 10:39; 16:25; Mk. 8:35; Lk. 9:24; 17:33). If we face such a challenge about the value of our lives, what claim do we have over the supposed sacredness of tradition?

Ritual

David Hogue recalls the church of his childhood and their conscious effort to avoid many common religious rituals. He describes the religious climate as "nonritualistic, or even antiritualistic."[10] For them, ritual meant nothing more than tireless recitation, void of any greater substance: spiritually-vacant tradition. The machinations of high church represented a stoic, aloof practice, which stood for all they intended to avoid.

Such repudiation distinguishes two concepts discussed in this chapter, by making a church tradition out of the rejection of ritual. This distinction helps draw a line between tradition and ritual and how they can operate separately. Hogue goes on to note that his church did fall into their own patterns of ritual over time, though they did not particularly align with the historical rituals of the Roman Catholic Church. Altar calls took place at the end of every service, always to the tune of the hymn, "Just as I Am." Though members of that church would reject this being labeled as a ritual, Hogue argues that it was. The association with the word *ritual* represents for them empty motions and meaningless words. Though altar calls may be less scripted than historical "high church" rituals, there is still power within the act, with the potential for both positive and negative effects.

Some believe that the call to the front for newly converted believers is the essence of the worship experience and, ultimately, the driving force behind their entire faith. However, for those who are not familiar with the practice, and particularly for those who may not already adhere to the same beliefs and values of the rest of the church, such rituals can come off as "intrusive, or even abusive."[11]

The rhythms of nature itself contain ritual patterns. Life is inhered with a sense of the sacred, which is expressed through ritual practice. It is a means by which we structure the world around us to help give it meaning. Catherine Bell describes ritual as "a 'window' on the cultural dynamics by which people make and remake their worlds."[12]

Ritual can mean many things to many people, and we can sometimes practice certain rituals without even being aware of it. Ritual without conscious intention can be powerful, but it also can be dangerous, particularly with respect to its ability to come across as exclusive or manipulative.

It is possible to stem the recklessness with which we employ rituals by carefully identifying, considering, and discussing the meaning behind the acts that we hold precious. Ritual, on a cultural level, is the mediator between the mind and body.[13] As such, ritual becomes an important way to bring people from a more abstracted, perhaps cerebral, experience of God, toward a more fully embodied worship experience. This cannot happen, though, without thoughtful and mutually respectful dialogue. Bell notes, "in the same way that ritual is seen to reintegrate thought and action in some form, discourse on ritual is seen to afford special access to cultural understanding by integrating the subject's thought and the object's activities."[14]

Do our rituals truly communicate what we think? What power, both positive and negative, do certain prayers, songs, images, and practices hold for those both within and outside our congregations? Too often, we fall into habits of worship, simply because there is little to shake us free of our tendency to fall into patterns of sameness. Sometimes, we hold desperately to traditions because we find some solace, or even power, in the maintenance of structures the way they always have been, such as firm gender roles within the church or rules about who may or may not participate in communion.

Ritualizing traditions have potential pitfalls, giving sanctity to patterns of behavior, not because they truly hold sacred value, but because they help reinforce existing power structures:

> Formalizing a gathering, following a fixed agenda and repeating that activity at periodic intervals, and so on, reveal potential strategies of ritualization because these ways of acting are the means by which one group of activities is set off as distinct and privileged vis-à-vis other activities. Yet in a different situation, informality might be stressed to dominate other ways of acting. For example, the formal activities of gathering for a Catholic mass distinguish this 'meal' from daily eating activities, but the informality of a mass celebrated in a private home with a folk guitar and kitchen utensils is meant to set up another contrast (the spontaneous authentic celebration versus the formal and inauthentic mass) which the informal service expects to dominate.[15]

Such a challenge begs many questions, such as: Is there a right or wrong way to observe communion? Are certain vestments truly necessary for worship to take place? Furthermore, are particular claims of faith, acts of stewardship, or church affiliation required to achieve spiritual salvation? We often scramble to justify those traditions we hold close, but if we truly seek to avail ourselves to a community already wary of our ways and expectations, we must fully understand all of our own behavior, separate tradition from ritual, and be able to articulate to each other and to those beyond our walls why we do what we do and why we believe it is an important part of the worship experience.

On the other hand, ritual and tradition can both emerge out of a reaction against previous ways of conducting worship. While many significant movements have found their roots in such rejoinders as the Protestant Reformation, we must be mindful that our new path is not simply guided by the absence of a perceived negative. In doing so, the thing we react against ultimately remains the force underlying our behavior in an antithetical way.

Whereas some have argued that many of the ways we express ourselves are genetically predetermined, evidence emerging in recent decades shows that such behavior is learned in a social environment. Bell considers the human body a "social construction in the image of society and a microcosm of the universe."[16]

In this way, our rituals express something about the community of faith, society as a whole, and the universe in general. This harkens back to Hogue's notion that ritual is inherent in the inner workings of the cosmos. In participating in ritual, then, we indeed may connect to something greater than ourselves. On an unspeakable level, such acts can help connect us to the more mystical nature of God. Through these embodied acts, we have an opportunity to bring the absent into the present, to make the abstract more concrete, to engage the human imagination as a vehicle for hope and for recognizing what is possible.

A Crisis of Imagination

In the first chapters of Genesis and the gospel of John, God utters the entirety of creation into existence. What also is implicit in this creative process is the preceding act of imagining what would be. Without first imagining the new creation to come, the words that follow would be empty and arbitrary. Though this idea places God within the context of human metaphors, it speaks to our understanding of the human organism. Without being driven by imagination, words and actions are without direction and ultimately without purpose.

In order to have a sense that one's life has meaning greater than the daily rigors that consume our minutes and hours, we must first acknowledge that we are "grounded in some greater reality."[17] Brent House, the Episcopal Center at the University of Chicago, offers some suggestions about how this meaning is evidenced, particularly for young adults. Its Web site states, "The meaning of one's life is derived from relationship. The relatedness of oneself as individual to the whole of life is invitation to an on-going conversation with all that constitutes the 'other.'"[18] Further, meaning as expressed within the Christian faith is found not in career, but rather in vocation. These two are not necessarily mutually exclusive, and some are fortunate to enjoy their vocation also as a profession.

This call, or vocation, for our own lives is found in the regular practice of seeking it out. We seek it in dialogue with one another, in intentional relationship, in silent prayer, in study of scripture, and in worship. All these acts have an opportunity to become sacred ritual, as they are part of a greater practice to connect with God. However, all these same behaviors can be conducted without the same intent to seek vocation and to connect with something greater. Taken a step further, these same actions can even become the very things that distract us from our greater purpose. Only in conceiving the possible first, and then acting in a manner that avails ourselves to a sense of calling and greater belonging, can we find the opportunity to experience the sacred.

For Jesus, truth is proclaimed everywhere, from the mouths of others to the silent whisper of nature (Lk. 19:40). It cannot be suppressed, but it can be ignored. Through individual and corporate practices of discernment, Christians engage in the ritual processes that attune us to this universal call, and we connect with something greater than ourselves.

Corporate rituals always have the potential for abuse and exclusion, as Hogue notes. For those who have negative associations with the rituals of church, the environment of worship suggests a hindrance to intimacy rather than an opportunity for it. As a child, Christian attended a Southern Baptist worship service with his grandparents. Baptists generally observe communion only four times a year. This particular Sunday happened to be a communion service, and Christian, who was nine years old at the time, asked to take part in the ritual. His grandparents explained he was not allowed. When he asked why, they explained that the church's policy was that you had to be a member of the church to participate in communion. Though he was a Baptist himself at the time, he was excluded from the sacred practice. While many in attendance may have found spiritual nourishment in the rites, Christian experienced alienation and a lingering sense of unworthiness.

Another possible cause of disconnection from ritual acts is a crisis of imagination. As discussed above, God's creation was not simply spoken into existence: It was first conceived, and then it was inspired. The Word was the means by which it was manifested, but the intent of what was to be created preceded the act of creation itself. As worshipers, we must imagine the intent of our engagement with ritual before participating, or else the words and motions have no evocative quality. Some have suggested that today's young adults, raised in an environment replete with video imagery, have never learned how to properly use their imaginations.

In a November 2006 issue of the *New Yorker,* Lara M. Brown, professor of political science at California State University–Channel Islands, decries the imaginative abilities of her students:

> This younger generation–raised on video games–has learned to be reactive instead of active, and worse, they have lost their imaginative abilities and creativity because the games provide all of the images, sounds and possible outcomes for them.[19]

Brown recognizes a general difficulty for her current students to generate questions or hypotheses. She believes this difficulty occurs because they are essentially waiting to see what happens next, rather than becoming agents in the process of dialogue and imagination. She expresses frustration when trying to evoke imaginary worlds for them, realizing that they struggle to envision absent times or places without the added medium of video to impart images to them. "In essence," she says, "they seem to have lost the ability to visualize with their minds."[20]

Ritual experiences presume a process of imagination. While we may not share the same symbolic meaning for each practice, the act itself is expected to represent some greater concept. This act is how we bring the absent into our presence, but if the ability to imagine the symbolic significance of the ritual is not there, the words and actions are void of any greater meaning other than the literal experience itself.

Story, Experience, and Ritual

How do we facilitate the imaginative process that brings sacred meaning to these rituals? The gospel of John suggests that creation itself is an ongoing dialogic process. For Christians, this process began with the Word that inspired creation, breathing life into the universe. It was brought to human form in the life of Jesus, and it was shared with future disciples through the gospel message. To presume that everyone comes around the table with the same understanding of the significance of rituals and traditions is assuming a lot. Even to expect that we all are able to find greater meaning in the acts of worship may be overstepping reality.

The Greek concept of *kairos* may help us to approach this disparity of understanding in a constructive way. Though difficult to translate literally into English, *kairos* can be understood as "in the fullness of time." It is a process-based concept, rather than an outcome-based one. University of Chicago's Brent House Web site offers some possible insight into the young adult experience of *kairos*:

> The conversation of vocation, the struggle to make meaning of one's life, seeks that quality which is *kairos*, that balance between fitness and readiness. One can be fit for a particular kind of work, but not yet ready to undertake it for lack of training or skill. One can be fit for a particular task, but not yet ready to undertake it for lack of physical prowess or emotional maturity. One can be fit for an intimate commitment, like marriage, but not yet ready to undertake it; or fit to conceive and bear children, but not yet ready to provide for their care and nurture. The process of discerning vocation is lifelong. Young adulthood is itself a moment of *kairos*.[21]

A community of faith is responsible for facilitating both the fitness and readiness of those who seek God's vocation in their lives. The church cannot expect that, simply because people show up, they are both fit and ready for the journey. Also, we must hold in mind and share with one another the importance of understanding that our experience of "fullness of time" is not a destination, but rather a trajectory toward which we direct ourselves, both individually and corporately. This journey happens best in ₁ safe environment that includes the opportunity for questions, supportive dialogue, and sharing our own stories of faith as well as what the rituals we practice mean to each of us.

If worship only harkens back to ancient times and absent places, it lacks relevance. If ritual is conducted without regard for our fitness and readiness, we lose an opportunity to experience a sacred moment. Hogue asserts that, "rituals become empty or hollow when they lose their connection with the original stories that set them in context. But perhaps more significantly, [they] lose their meaning when they become disconnected from our own personal stories."[22]

Ritual offers many opportunities. It does not provide them automatically, but placed in the proper context and connected to the stories both of our past and present, it opens the way to the greater connection that we seek in a lifelong faith experience. Executed well, a ritual lifts up a time and place, making it sacred. It provides order in a chaotic life, and it moves us forward. The act of repetition, when combined with proper intentional planning and preparation, can serve to deepen a spiritual encounter.[23] Adequate planning and preparation presume a degree of fitness and readiness on the part of those leading us in the act.

We also must be open to the multitude of experiences provided by ritual. People have many experiences and expressions of God. For each of us to take something different away from a ritual act is not a sign of failure, but rather in indication of the creativity of the Holy Spirit working within each of us uniquely, and at the same time, among us all.

Finally, we must consider not only the inevitability, but the necessity for the liminal experience of young adulthood. For those feeling neither here nor there, being a young adult can feel disquieting and full of despair. However, the concept of liminality, though not grounded in the present, suggests something at the threshold. It is the experience of kairos. It implies the potential for change, the creative potential of all that is possible, and the open-ended nature of a future founded in hope. What is most difficult about embracing a liminal experience is that we sometimes must set down old ways and identities in order to discover new ones. This process is terrifying and unstable by its very nature. A community of faith, when at its best, is an agent of transformation. This transformation is not always without discomfort and fear of the unknown, but by our presence, and by sharing our own experiences of surviving such liminality, we demonstrate that many who have gone down this path before have lived to tell about it.

Hogue states that there are many ways to visualize how story, ritual, and experience are related. In one model, stories inform ritual acts, leading to an experience that connects back to a tangible connection with these defining stories:

STORY ⟶ RITUAL ⟶ EXPERIENCE[24]

Sometimes, from our life experiences emerge new rituals, which in turn inform our shared stories. In this case, the relationship between the three might be imagined more like this:

EXPERIENCE ⟶ RITUAL ⟶ STORY[25]

A third, and perhaps most accurate, way of understanding the relationship with regard to practical application is a more organic, less linear model:

STORY ⟷ RITUAL[26] / EXPERIENCE

Ideally, personal experience brings to life the stories of one's faith ancestry, making relevant the ancient messages of biblical texts. Faith provides a context within which daily life has some sense of order and meaning. This process can be facilitated by the intimate exchange of stories and the shared practice of sacred ritual.

In this climate of communal stories and mutual trust, believers can develop a spiritual fitness and an emotional readiness that prepares us to let go of those things which give us our present identity, giving ourselves up to sacred moments, allowing ourselves to be inspired by God's call. Ritual is a means of both grounding us in a history greater than our current condition and also contextualizing present life. Without the backdrop of stories of faith, ritual lacks meaning and substance.

Stories lose the power to connect us with God without the intentional discipline of ritual. Experience, stories, and ritual are a three-legged stool, all parts of which must act in concert to create the sacred time and space we seek in a community of faith.

Rites of Passage

Personality theorist Gordon Allport suggests that religion is expressed in many ways. In fundamental terms, intrinsic religion is a personally embraced, heartfelt experience of faith, whereas extrinsic religion is a utilitarian approach that uses religion as a means of bolstering one's social status or perceived righteousness.[27] Allport also compares mature and immature religious sentiment, with the former characterized by dynamic, open-minded approaches to faith, and the latter identified with self-serving attitudes, often conforming to the negative stereotypes about religion.[28]

Ideally, as believers we all wish to offer an intrinsic, mature faith experience relevant to one's daily life, while also reaching beyond direct experience to expand our spiritual and theological perspective. In his book, *The Individual and His Religion,* Allport offers several traits of a religious system that facilitates healthy personal development:[29]

1. *Differentiated:* Relevant contemporary faith communities must incorporate reason into their theology. The religious climate should encourage and facilitate questions and discourse and should also welcome a variety of scriptural and theological understandings.
2. *Dynamic:* Faith rooted only in the past risks becoming irrelevant to a society seeking a faith they can take into the world with them.
3. *Consistent Morality:* The messages of the church should not simply focus on so-called moral messages (abortion, homosexuality), but must also tackle justice issues (homelessness, genocide, ecology) and must present a call to action and an impetus for social change.
4. *Integral and Comprehensive:* The words and deeds of the faith community cannot come across as contradictory. This stems first and foremost from the actions of church leadership, who model the values for the congregation.
5. *Heuristic:* The theology of a faith community cannot be built on a closed set of doctrines. To help promote healthy personal development, the church should be eager to seek new insight, rather than simply confirming and buttressing existing views. In short, the church must be willing to grow and change.[30]

We must, then, facilitate both the fitness and readiness of our faith community, helping people to navigate their lives as empowered, sentient Christians. They must believe that the spiritual nourishment they receive is sufficient to sustain them in the ethically-barren social landscape. Our strength comes not only from our conviction in word but also in deed, and our relevance emerges as we avail ourselves to the issues with which they are struggling. We must patiently cultivate each individual's spiritual growth, careful not to conform them to our own understanding, but rather allowing them to develop a personal spiritual wisdom through experience, study, prayer, and community.

Theologian James Fowler elaborates on Allport's concept of immature and mature faith, explicating six distinct stages of faith development. In the first stages we constantly shift between trust and anxiety as infants to adopting religious ideas from our family of origin. As we are introduced to a faith community, we begin to learn and ascribe to the social values and moral rules of the group.

The fourth stage is the critical point for youth and young adults, and it is the point at which many churches begin to fail their young people. Fowler says in this stage of life that we begin to take personal ownership of and develop an identity with the religious heritage of our faith. If this occurs in a relevant, healthy, dynamic way, it contributes greatly to the person's emotional stability, and it facilitates a deep sense of belonging.[31]

Conceptually, this process makes sense, but how do we go about it? Most Christian churches, particularly Protestants, have lost a connection with any meaningful rites of passage for our children and young adults. We celebrate baptisms and claims of faith, but as far as acknowledging the natural progress of physical, emotional, psychic, and spiritual maturation, we aren't really sure what to do once our kids reach high school. If we are at a loss about what to do with teenagers, we are piteously ill-equipped to handle the unique spiritual needs of college-age adults and thirtysomethings.

Some churches still hold confirmation classes for school-age children, but the practical fitness and readiness these kids receive to manage life on their own is sparse to nonexistent. Starting at least by the time children reach their teenage years, if not before, we must commit to being more proactive about raising them up as spiritually, emotionally, and mentally strong members of society.

At the United Church of Santa Fe (UCC) in New Mexico, Rev. Talitha Arnold has introduced an eighteen-month-long program for junior high and high school students called, "Self, Society, Spirituality, and Sexuality." Male and female coleaders run the program, which includes classes, mission trips, and perhaps most important, matches each young person with an adult mentor who will lead them through the program throughout the year-and-a-half session.

"Choosing the right mentor can go a long way toward making this program meaningful for the kids," says Alissa Reyes, United's minister for children and youth. "Through a lot of planning, and just plain luck, we matched the right kids with the right adults this time around."[32] The entire group participates in a weeklong mission trip, where they work serving the poor, and once a month they commit to a local service project together.

Before the program even begins, participants and their families take part in a "Rite of Separation" service, in which parents symbolically say goodbye to their children (to their childhood), and children are paired with their mentors for the next eighteen months. Students and mentors meet at least once every six weeks throughout the program to discuss everything from school and social pressures to theological issues, family struggles, or questions about personal identity.

For the service projects, parents of the kids, as well as their mentors and other church members, are strongly encouraged to join the group in service, helping to model the communal commitment to service. The group then spends the first week of Holy Week in Washington, D.C., with their mentors, worshiping on Palm Sunday at the National Cathedral. While there, they meet with legislators and other government officials to discuss pressing social issues on the state, national, and global levels. The trip concludes with a tour of the Holocaust Museum.[33]

Throughout the year, classes focus on different social issues related to the experiences of the youth. A safe, open environment is cultivated within the group to allow for intimate sharing and questioning. Subjects range from sexuality to drugs, future plans, and spiritual identity. As the youth move through the class, they are prepared to offer testimonials to the congregation, articulating their own spiritual beliefs to the community that has supported them through the protracted journey.[34]

At the end of the program, each participant is called forward with their parents, and another ceremony is conducted in which the family says good-bye to the young person's childhood and welcomes them as adult members of the congregation. As a first act of service to the church, the new confirmands serve communion to the whole church.[35]

We have examples of similar rites of passage in our culture, though each addresses contemporary social issues by varying degrees. The Jewish tradition of Bar Mitzvahs and Bat Mitzvahs are often observed for youth as they turn thirteen years old. Many Hispanic cultures observe the *Quinceañera,* a party thrown for a young woman's fifteenth birthday to acknowledge her transition into womanhood. However, the concept of formal rites of passage for young people has largely been lost in modern American culture. If it is recognized, it is in a diluted form, such as "coming out" parties and debutante balls. Depicted on television shows such as *My Sweet Sixteen,* these increasingly popular festivities are elaborate displays of affluence, placing the teenager on a pedestal for all to coddle and adore. Though they may enjoy attention and material outpouring at the time, this hardly prepares them for the rigors and vicissitudes of the "real world."

Sex and Money

CLER Ministries is a nonprofit, Bible-based sexuality education program affiliated with the Christian Church (Disciples of Christ). The program is far more comprehensive than an abstinence-only position. The curriculum begins as early as elementary school, with programs that include increasing levels of sophistication and detail, and continues through adulthood. Subjects include anatomy, degrees of arousal, self-care, sexually transmitted diseases, and various biblical foundations for building relationships based upon love and lifelong commitment.[36]

Participants are allowed to ask any questions they want, as long as they are sincere. There is no shame in discussing one's sexuality. Instead, young people learn to both understand and respect their bodies, so that they are prepared to deal with the vagaries of adolescence and all that comes along with it when it arrives. The organization, developed and managed by Linda and Richard Goddard, also offers weeklong camp programs for seventh grade students in place of their annual church camp experience.[37] The curriculum strongly encourages churches to continue the dialogue throughout the student's tenure at the church. Throughout the process, they learn that, though sex is not something to be feared and their bodies are not something of which they should be ashamed, both should be respected and understood.

Another equally powerful and equally misunderstood commodity is money. We emerged from college with a combined six-figure student debt load and close to $10,000 in credit card debt. Meanwhile, Amy worked part-time in ministry as she made her way through seminary, while Christian worked as a grant writer at a local nonprofit. The prospect for a stable, solvent financial future was grim for a young married couple intent on following less than lucrative career paths. Money was always a point of stress and often became the focal point of our arguments.

Around our fifth anniversary our former marriage counselor, Gay Hatler, the senior pastor at First Christian Church (DOC) in Colorado Springs, gave us a call.

"How are things going for you guys?" he asked.

"Fine, good, great, all right," we wavered.

"Fighting about money yet?"

"Yeah," we confessed. "It's pretty tight these days." Two or three times a year, we were overdrawing our bank account, juggling bills, and making minimum payments on revolving debt, just to keep from getting into deeper trouble.

"Why don't you come by and see me," he said. "I have a program I want to show you." Hatler walked us through a program by Dave Ramsey called Financial Peace University. Hatler's church had taught the class on Bible-based financial planning several times with overwhelming success. We agreed to purchase the starter kit for $100 and give the program a try for three months.

We have now been on the Financial Peace plan for almost two years. In that time, we have paid off one student loan, all of our credit cards, and both car loans. We established life insurance policies and long-term disability insurance plans, as well as a college fund for our three-year-old son. We also have a cash reserve nearly equal to the cushion we had by employing our credit cards before. However, now, instead of paying 18 to 21 percent interest for the security, we receive 5 to 8 percent interest on our reserve.

All this begs the question: Why didn't we learn this sooner?

It's no surprise, really. Our parents all struggled with their finances, with some filing bankruptcy, and others living out of their car for a period of time. Not only was sound financial discipline not modeled for us, but we also fell in love with the message imparted by the secular world when we ventured out on our own: credit is a sign of maturity; having debt means you're a real adult.

We now realize that the inevitability of a life bound to debt is a lie spread throughout modern culture. It is an insidious epidemic that not only runs counter to biblical principles (Prov. 22:7) but is a recipe for strained relationships, distorted values, and unrealistic expectations. Last year, we taught a Financial Peace class for the first time at our church. This year, we have had such a great demand for another class that we will likely have to move into our sanctuary to accommodate everyone.

While the adult class is valuable, it is hardly proactive in most cases. As parents, we should be taking on the responsibility of teaching fiscal accountability and generosity from the time we start giving children an allowance. To this end, Ramsey offers several programs, from Junior's Clubhouse for kids, Financial Peace for the Next Generation for schools, and No Matter What for teens.[38]

We will address the need for, and benefit of, twelve-step groups in our chapter on addiction, but the issues raised above are only a few of the issues our churches should be concerned about. By cultivating healthy living habits, we engender a tradition of spiritual wholeness into our faith culture. In recognizing rites of passage and walking step by step alongside our youth, we make sacred the milestones they face, assuring them they must not face them alone. We nurture a foundation for dialogue and a sense of empowerment that affords young adults the fitness and readiness they require to enter a world replete with mixed messages, false hopes, and distorted principles.

Addiction

College, Catharsis, Crisis *(As Told by Christian)*

I loved college. I still look back on those years as some of the most exciting years of my life, in both good ways and bad. They are also the years when I came most saliently face-to-face with my own mortality. In high school, I was a relatively "good" kid. As a musician, I hung out with plenty of people who lived more adventurously than I did, but I was content at the time to stand by and observe in fascination.

By the time I got to college, however, I began to see the world as much bigger and more complex than I had previously understood it. I met people whose values and experiences stretched my understanding of normality. I ran with poets, deadheads, bohemians, anarchists, and tortured prodigies. I drank, smoked, snorted, and swallowed any number of substances in a romantic endeavor to press the limits of physical consciousness. I played music, discussed literature, slept late, stayed up until sunrise, and lived according to my own ever-shifting standards.

I took a job with a major record company in Dallas, where I met yet another subculture of hedonistic, artistic, sometimes altruistic, but generally masochistic dilettantes. Most of the people with whom I worked were what I would have then called "posers" or "wannabes," clinging to the garments of other people's fame like a security blanket. Few of them had any artistic spark of their own, yet they were content to warm themselves by the artistic fires of others.

Part of my job was to offer hospitality to touring musicians. I was supposed to make sure they were comfortable while in town, and to make sure they had a good time while not on stage. For a young college student, a job like this was like manna from heaven. I was comped free drinks in some bars for bringing famous people there, and I had a pass at other clubs for keeping the staff supplied with plenty of free music. One evening, the Dave Matthews Band was in town, playing at a local club called Trees. The representative from RCA Records, Dave's label, opened a line of credit at the bar for the band and our support staff. Every time I walked by, he handed me another tequila shot. I hated tequila, but I could actually have been criticized for turning down drinks from a client, so I accepted.

After the show, the RCA rep pulled several of us onto Dave's bus. It was like a nightclub on wheels. Had they given me the opportunity, I would gladly have given up my apartment to live in it all of the time. Dave and the rest of the band were in the back, cooling off after their sets. We were introduced and made small talk, though by then I was drunk enough that I don't recall any of what was discussed. A combination of alcohol, starstruck awe, and anxiety about looking stupid rendered me nearly mute. I was so uneasy and nervous that I hardly remember anything about the experience.

The next day, my supervisor called me into her office. She said she wanted to ask me about some "disturbing things" that had happened on Dave's bus. I began to sweat, and my cheeks flushed with fear as I tried to recall any prurient details through the gauze of a lingering hangover. As I took a seat and she closed the door behind us, I waited for the inevitable ax to fall. Fortunately for me, the swinging blade was not meant for my neck. Apparently, one of our interns brought his uninvited girlfriend on the bus, and she then proceeded to sit on the lap of every band member. When asked to leave, she refused, resulting in more assertive means of diplomacy to escort them to the street. Though I had been on the bus at the time, I couldn't remember enough to confirm or deny the details of the event. All I could tell her was that I saw them on board.

This incident was a close call, but it was hardly enough to indicate anything of concern about my behavior to me at the time. After all, the label took us on trips to clubs in New York and Austin to do more of the same over the next couple of years. If anything, the cycle of excess and subsequent remorseful anxiety became a more acceptable way of life.

We regularly made the rounds of the local bars back in Denton where we lived, all of which were within two blocks of each other. We could park our cars at my friend's house, walk to the strip, drink our fill, stumble back to his place, and crash on the couch until lunchtime the next day. Beer was so cheap that even I, with my part-time music gig, could afford enough to catch a buzz any night of the week. Most of the bars featured a thirty-two–ounce cup called a chugger, which cost $2.80 at the time. For $10, I could throw back a couple of chuggers, get a friend or two to buy a round of shots, hit the after-parties at the local lodge, and still have enough left over for a greasy stop at Whataburger to help soak up the liquor.

Thursday evenings were the big party nights in Denton. It was a commuter school, so a lot of people went back home on the weekends. Generally, we started our rounds on Wednesday, considering this the warm-up night for the week, then we'd hit all of the parties and shows on Thursday. Friday and Saturday were generally reserved for shows in Dallas, trailing bands from one of the labels for whom I worked or playing shows of my own. Sunday usually ended up being a laid-back day for beer, barbecue, and a little bit of rest.

It never occurred to me that this meant I was drinking steadily upwards of five nights out of every week. It's just what we did. I even got paid to do it, so how could it be a problem?

One evening we decided to make our way to my friend's sister's house to see if she had anything to drink after the bars closed. She welcomed us in as she always did, more than used to intrusive visits from both of us by that time. She lived in a two-story townhome, with the bathroom at the top of at least twenty stairs. I made my way carefully upstairs, but the couch for which I was bound next was back by the front door. My brain evidently had more confidence in my legs' ability to navigate the stairs than they deserved, because I slipped near the top and fell in a sort of barrel roll to the entryway at the bottom.

I blacked out for a minute, aroused by what felt like someone tickling the end of my nose. As I finally got my bearings, I realized the tickle was a steady stream of blood, dripping from my forehead across my face. I had hit my head hard enough against the stairs and wall to give myself a concussion. This injury, combined with the alcohol in my system, caused me to begin vomiting violently. As I sat in a pool of my own blood and puke, my friend and his sister urged me to go to the hospital. I refused, explaining that I didn't have insurance, but the root of my refusal was shame. I knew if I went to the emergency room, I'd have to explain how I ended up like this.

My parents would likely have been called, and they would freak out. I decided that I'd rather take my chances on the couch, with a towel pressed against my forehead, than deal with the embarrassment.

The next day, I felt about as bad as I could have without being dead. My forehead was swollen and bruised, and I could hardly move without feeling nauseous. For the next couple of weeks, I could not tilt my head back without getting so dizzy that I had to sit down. For me, this experience was my so-called "rock bottom." People in recovery talk about how each person has to find his or her own low point. This will either serve as a wake-up call, or be the point of no return. I decided that my life was worth more than a few lines in the obituaries about how I died falling down a flight of stairs at age twenty.

I am one of the lucky ones. Once I decided I had gone too far, I was able to attenuate my behavior. For many, the grip of addiction takes hold, draining their will and occluding their ability to see anything other than their present state of hopelessness. I still have the scar on my forehead from the fall. In a way, not getting stitches was a healthy reminder for me. Had the scar healed too well, I might not have such a prominent reminder of my own potential for addiction. That's not something I want to forget.

The Human Condition

We are born both with the capacity to love and the potential to do evil. Humans are the agents for compassion and indifference in the world. Without us, neither compassion nor indifference has any potency or potential to be realized. This reality is the source of a great deal of suffering.

Paul illustrates this plight best in the seventh chapter of his letter to the church in Rome:

> I do not understand my own actions. For I do not do what I want, but I do the very thing I hate…For I do not do the good I want, but the evil I do not want is what I do…Wretched man that I am! Who will rescue me from this body of death?[1]

Coming to terms with being loved can be difficult in itself, but accepting that people choose suffering and are the source of the pain is an obstacle we spend a lifetime trying to surmount.

Here, Paul sounds less like a great apostle and more like someone in a twelve-step group. Imagine how different this epistle might have been had he been in recovery. The element of Paul's writing that we will focus on now is the real, human element of addiction. "Addiction is characterized by the repeated use of substances or behaviors despite clear evidence of morbidity secondary to such use. The American Heritage Stedman's Medical Dictionary defines addiction as 'Habitual psychological or physiological dependence on a substance or practice beyond one's voluntary control.'"[2] This is a fancy way of saying that, despite the best human efforts, we often do not do the thing we want, but the thing we hate.

Doing What We Hate

Regardless of the object of Paul's attachment to sin, his struggle is like our own. His salvation rests in the same hands. His faith points in the same direction: to God. The beauty and success of twelve-step programs are found in their members' willingness to be honest and open to help from a Higher Power. The first three of the twelve steps in Alcoholics Anonymous reveal an underlying theme of surrendering to God:

- Step 1. We admitted we were powerless over alcohol—that our lives had become unmanageable.
- Step 2. We came to believe that a Power greater than ourselves could restore us to sanity.
- Step 3. We made a decision to turn our wills and our lives over to the care of God as we understood Him.[3]

At some point, the addict has to choose between her or his own way and God's. "The solution to the human dilemma is…to rely on God's grace revealed in Jesus Christ and to live in the power of the Holy Spirit given by God to all Christians…[and] represents the objective situation of the person apart from Christ, who can never extricate himself or herself from the world's evil and from personal sin by his or her own efforts."[4]

Scholars have argued for years about the behavior Paul refers to. Some believe he is referring to a deep-seated depression, while others believe it is guilt. Some argue he is struggling with plain old sin. In *The People's New Testament Commentary*, M. Eugene Boring and Fred Craddock title it simply, "The Inner Conflict." Whatever the case, Paul sounds like an addict. More important, he sounds like us. If we have nothing else in common, we can always commiserate over our inability to overcome sin, at least on our own.

Steps to Recovery

Step one is universal. Take out "alcohol" and replace it with any number of other addictive substances or behaviors: We admitted we were powerless over sex, food, gambling, spending, cigarettes, and so on and that our lives had become unmanageable. Twelve-step groups work because people are free to tell the truth in a room full of people who sympathize and often empathize with their stories. As a result we learn we are not alone. "In any meeting, anywhere, A.A.'s share experience, strength, and hope with each other, in order to stay sober and help other alcoholics… A.A.'s speak the language of the heart in all its power and simplicity."[5] Church, at its best, serves people in a similar way. It provides people with a safe place to share their story and to be embraced, loved, and forgiven as children of God who are not alone in the world.

Alcoholics Anonymous, however, has spread its message more successfully in recent years. The "fourth edition of 'Alcoholics Anonymous' came off the press in November 2001, at the start of a new millennium. Since the third edition was published in 1976, worldwide membership of AA has nearly doubled, to an estimated two million or more, with nearly 100,800 groups meeting in approximately 150 countries around the world."[6] Obviously, AA is on to something. They are growing faster than most churches, and their overall impact on society is immeasurable.

There is no magic bullet when it comes to church growth. Authentic witness takes time. We can look to the Traditions of AA for guidance here as well: "Tradition Eleven—our public relations policy is based on attraction rather than promotion."[7] The best case we can make for church is to be a people who sincerely love and serve within a vital community of faith. No advertising gimmick or evangelism tactic will work to get young adults to church as well as face-to-face visits.

This requires vulnerability on our part and on the part of those on whom we call. Too often the pastoral/lay visitation is viewed as a thirty-minute window through which we must cram every tidbit of information about our church programs and theology. What if we reenvision this time as an opportunity to be present to a person in need? Do we have everything they need? Of course not. But we do have the capacity to listen deeply and respond with love and authenticity.

An Addiction Epidemic

Love is a good place to start, especially when we consider the complex lives with which we come into contact. According to the National Department of Health and Human Services, rates of substance dependence or abuse are prevalent among young adults:

> In 2005, 21.8 percent [of] young adults aged 18 to 25 had higher rates of substance dependence or abuse than adults aged 26 or older (7.1 percent). Among persons with substance dependence or abuse, the proportion dependent on or abusing illicit drugs was associated with age. In 2005, 58.2 percent of youths aged 12 to 17, 38.6 percent of young adults aged 18 to 25, and 22.3 percent of adults aged 26 or older with substance dependence or abuse were dependent on or abused illicit drugs."[8]

The need for resources offering intervention and treatment for young adults is obvious. "In 2005, among young adults aged 18 to 25, the rate of binge drinking was 41.9 percent, and the rate of heavy drinking was 15.3 percent."[9] Nearly half of young adults are binge drinking and nearly one seventh of them are heavy drinkers. Alcoholics face three possible outcomes to their addiction: death, incarceration, or recovery. We have a choice: We can either wait to do their funerals or we can help them and their families now. Where is the church? Today, we are far more involved in funeral planning than we are in intervention and treatment.

What if we were able to say to them, "I too am an addict," or, "We suffer from the same disease"? What if, instead of turning our heads to the addicts in all of our lives, churches provided meeting places for twelve-step groups, intervention teams in our congregations, and recovery literature in our libraries? At the very least we can be honest about our own addictions. We can model recovery and live into the hope of a God who can restore us to sanity.

Church can make a real difference for people suffering from addiction. "Intervention services are the best way to make help available to those struggling with an addiction. Ninety-two percent of those intervened on go to treatment and have the opportunity to change their lives."[10] This is good news. First, we need to get over the antiquated notion that addicts are all homeless people sleeping in gutters, clutching a bottle. Yes, these people exist, and they need our help and love as well. But the majority of the practicing addicts in the world are semi-productive, functional members of society. They are business owners, accountants, teachers, ministers, politicians, and bank tellers. They are you and I.

A comprehensive approach to recovery for everyone affected by the addict's behavior is the most genuine gesture of love we can extend to an addict and their loved ones. Intervention is essential to the recovery process. The impact is far-reaching. If we wait too long, however, we may lose the opportunity:

> An intervention is a structured, solution-focused process that consists of a group of close friends, family members and others (coworkers, colleagues, spiritual advisors, etc.) who come together in a caring and non-judgmental manner to present their observations and concerns regarding an addict's behavior. A well-executed intervention is professionally facilitated and aims to move the family or workplace system out of crisis and assists in immediately addressing addiction.[11]

> After the intervention [people need to be] available for... consultations, whether or not the individual chooses to accept help for his or her problem, [and for] helping [everyone involved to] start [their] own path of recovery and healing.[12]

We are not responsible for other people's recovery. However, we do claim responsibility for guiding them toward their own path of recovery and healing. We offer this through honesty, compassion, and being available for the addict and his or her family as they seek the wholeness they have lost.

Our Family Intervention *(As Told by Amy)*

My fears in sharing this story are that no one will believe me, that it will seem sensationalized or dramatic, and that I will embarrass my family.

My job is not to worry about how it will be received or what people will think. My job is to tell the truth. If I am going to preach the truth, I must practice it.

Drunk driving killed my uncle when I was four years old. He was one of a number of practicing alcoholics in my family at the time, but he paid the highest price. He was nineteen. He was driving when he lost control of his car and drove into a drainage culvert. The water, they say, was only deep enough to cover the car. He and the young man in the car with him both drowned. It would be years before my family sobered up, but we could no longer deny the disease that was killing us.

When a policeman met my father at the door, he knew what had happened to his brother before the cop told him. Donnie was dead. My father did what any alcoholic would do in this situation: he drank. He went, on the morning of Donnie's death, with his only other living brother to the dump. They were there to collect Donnie's personal belongings from the car. Along with his wallet and a few photos they found a half-empty bottle of vodka in the back seat. They brought the bottle home and drank the rest of the alcohol that had contributed to his death. "To Don," they said, and finished the vodka.

That's addiction. The image of the two of them raising their glasses will remain in my memory forever. If I forget it, I risk losing also the lessons that this pain taught our family.

Seven years later, finally, the pain was so great that we surrendered and got help. A lifelong friend of the family came for a visit. Somehow, he was different. He was sober. He shared with us the hope he had discovered in rehab and asked us if we wanted it for ourselves. This conversation was the beginning of our recovery, all because one individual was willing to face his own addictions and share his newfound serenity with others.

Finding healing and sharing it with others are how we as the church can make a difference. This is our intervention. We must come to terms with our own addictions and get honest about our shortcomings. Let us choose recovery. The world needs us. People are suffering. Only God can rescue us from this body bound by death. Let us decide together to turn our wills and our lives over to the care of God. We will find, and give, new life.

A couple of years ago, I went to an open AA meeting with my dad. He was celebrating his seventeenth year of sobriety. Instead of having him speak, they asked me to share. I looked around the room and saw people who had found peace, and who had helped others find it as well. I said simply, "Thank you." My dad was presented with his seventeen-year "chip," which is really a coin, with the "Serenity Prayer" printed on one side and the Roman numerals "XVII" on the other. He took it, and then he gave it to me.

I keep that chip with me. It serves as a reminder of all that my family has taught me about facing the truth as a means to healing. It also reminds me to humbly seek the grace that I am called to share with the world. It ensures that I will never forget the power addiction has to destroy lives. This gives me compassion for others who have yet to find recovery, and compels me to help them discover it.

Jake's Story

Jake's desire for meaningful community has been a theme throughout his life. The ways in which he has sought it, however, varied widely. At age fifteen, he fell in with a circle of friends who held keg parties on the weekends. Jake notes that drinking was equivalent to acceptance among his peers, and so he went along with the group norm. Before he was old enough to drive, he was smoking weed and drinking on a regular basis.

Even in Jake's younger years, he made at least half-hearted efforts to manage his chemical dependence. He went to drug rehab for the first time when he was seventeen, though he admits that the only thing he quit at the time was school. His counselor in rehab warned him that, if he did not change his course of behavior, he would either be dead or in prison within the year. Emboldened by the immortality of youth, Jake considered this a sort of challenge.

Neither this warning nor the other programs he experienced during rehab did much to stem his interest in drugs. He notes that of the four friends with whom he partied the most during those years, the other two who went to rehab both ended up in jail, while the two who didn't get admitted eventually stopped on their own, going on to raise families and pursue careers.

Following his first stint in a recovery program, Jake expanded his experimentation with drugs to include the hallucinogenic LSD, or acid. Around the same time, his girlfriend was killed in a car wreck, and his roommate was severely injured, spending several months in the hospital. The driver of the car, who was unhurt, moved in with Jake into a one-bedroom apartment, which soon became the party headquarters for their friends. Over time, more people started crashing there, until five of them shared the cramped space. None of them had a job, so they would keep themselves supplied with drugs by trading stolen cigarettes to a local dealer for hits of acid.

"I have heard some say that after five hits of LSD you are considered insane," says Jake, "[but] I once ate over twenty [hits] in a single day." Subsisting on candy bars and white toast, he would trip several times a week, with each trip lasting up to eight hours.

Desperate for money to keep a roof over their heads and drugs in their pockets, they turned to burglary. Jake notes that most of the people they robbed were people they knew, but the urge to avoid sobriety was stronger than any guilt they might experience. Near the end of his year out of rehab, he recognized he was on the verge of fulfilling his counselor's predictions. As an act of desperation, he returned to his parents' house to seek their help in returning to treatment. They were out of town, but Jake didn't know where else to go, so he broke in and waited. After a shower and a nap, he began to worry that whoever was watching their house for them might find him there and mistake him for an intruder. Rather than risk having to explain his presence, he grabbed his mother's car keys, a jar of change, and a stash of his dad's guns. He and his friend Kyle had talked about taking off for California for weeks, so Jake picked him up and headed west.

They only made it as far as Vegas before their money ran out, so they resorted to stealing gas wherever they could. In Phoenix, they traded some of the guns for cocaine and went on a binge. "I don't know how long we were there," he says. "It might have been a week, might have been a month." One day bled into another as they converted more stolen goods into drugs, living off of the oranges they pilfered from a local grove. When he was finally arrested, two months after his eighteenth birthday, he had thirty-six warrants out for his arrest. He was considered an armed and dangerous criminal.

Over the next six years, Jake was only out of jail for eight months. He was paroled one time, released on bond another, and escaped once as well. It never took long, however, for him to fall back into his old patterns of behavior. "Every chance I got I jumped back into the same old shit," he says. "Even in prison I would get high every chance I got. Looking back I think a big part of it had to do with that sense of community, the friendships, the acceptance, the excitement, and of course getting high feels really good. That's how so many people get hooked."

In 1994, Jake completed his sentence and found the first stable job he had ever held. He recalls the sense of comfort he found in having his own place, paying all of his bills, and hanging out with a couple of "good" friends. Despite his new life, he still smoked pot daily and frequented bars most evenings after work. Within a couple of years, boredom set in, and Jake got restless. He got a call from Scott, an old friend who was stranded in Castle Rock and was looking for a place to hide out. Scott had gotten mixed up with some "crackheads" and wanted to lay low, somewhere out of town for a while. On the way back, Jake and Scott decided to pick up an "eight ball" of cocaine (an eighth of an ounce), just like old times.

At first, Jake convinced himself he was in control of his cocaine habit, indulging only on weekends. Before long, he realized he was thinking about smoking coke, called freebasing, throughout the week, which made him nervous. Instead of backing off, Jake switched to crank, a form of speed that can be snorted or smoked. Though crank is much cheaper than cocaine, the high can last for several hours. For someone growing short on money, it was the perfect substitute.

"It was great times at first," he says. "I had great friends and pretty girls hanging around. We would party all night Friday, stay at the bar until sometimes six or seven the next morning [since] the bartender was a friend, [and] we didn't have to leave at closing time. All day Saturday, Saturday night, [and] through Sunday afternoon were part of the same party. Sometimes Sunday night sleep did not come until three or four in the morning, [which] made it necessary to do a bit more to be at work by six in the morning."

This pattern carried on for six months, until he had missed so much work that he was at risk of losing his job. He was also several months behind on rent because he was spending all of his money on drugs and alcohol, so as a last-ditch effort to avoid the inevitable, he returned to rehab. In doing so, he elicited sympathy from his employer and landlord, both of whom worked with Jake to keep him from losing everything. The six-week program was outpatient, which he remembers as "a joke." Within two weeks of completing the program, he was using again.

Jake hooked up with a new dealer, who provided him with speed far superior to anything he had ever tried before. Naturally, he shared his new find with a few others, and soon word began to spread. Though Jake had never bought more than $100 at one time, he got more requests for drugs every day. Before long he was buying and selling up to a quarter-pound of crank a day. He could buy a daily supply for $3,200 and sell it for nearly $5,000. Meanwhile, he kept himself flush with as many drugs as he could stand for personal use, and the money kept flowing in.

Finally, Jake succumbed to the idea that he was a drug addict. However, instead of using this realization as motivation to seek recovery, it was the excuse he needed to keep using. "I remember it as clear as if it were yesterday," he says, recalling the day he decided to give up. "Since I was a drug addict and could not get–or stay–sober, I would instead be a drug addict. I would use without guilt or remorse, always reminding myself that I got high because it was fun and I liked the people. If it got to the point that it was no longer fun," he told himself, "I would quit."

The next three years blended together in a haze of drugs, sleepless nights, and parties. Jake tried any drug he came across that he didn't have to inject, and over time, he lost everything. Even his more hard-core friends put distance between themselves and him in an effort to stave off a similar fate. With no home, car, or job, Jake did whatever he had to do in order to survive. "I only had one passion–getting high," says Jake. "It consumed all my attention, all my resources, all my time." He would stay awake often for days at a time, slipping in and out of hallucinogenic states. At one point, he recalls not sleeping for four straight weeks. Eventually, he could not discern the difference between real experience and hallucinations.

In the winter of 1999, Jake was living in the garage of his friend's mother. He gave her money for rent when he could scrape some together, and he continued to deal drugs. His parents called and offered to take him to his grandparents' apartment for Christmas. Because he felt bad for missing Thanksgiving all together, he agreed. The person they saw hardly resembled the boy they had once known. At six-foot-two, he weighed only 130 pounds. He had not slept in at least a week, having been up smoking speed. "I am not sure if I even showered or put on clean clothes," he says. "I don't remember much of [that] night."

The one thing he does recall was being joined by his aunt downstairs while he shared a smoke with his uncle. Knowing she was a Christian, Jake figured he'd strike up a conversation about spirituality. "I explained to her about astrology, tarot cards, and how I thought I was psychic," he says, citing his beliefs to her as the reason why he was still alive and currently out of jail. In response, she asked him if he knew how many people had been praying for him over the past several years. "It was the first time anybody offered an explanation that made sense," he says. "I had so many near-misses, so many times that circumstances put me out of harm's way, that I could not deny that something supernatural had been happening in my life. I explained it by psychic powers because I had no other answer."

When he awoke in the garage with the rest of his "tweaker" friends the next day, things seemed different. As he scanned the leaks in the roof and piles of animal excrement on the floor, a mouse fell from the ceiling onto his head. The garage had no toilets or showers, and his bags showed signs of others rummaging through them. True to form, he decided to numb out with drugs, but their effect had changed. "No matter how much I did, I couldn't get high," he says, "at least not high enough to have fun."

Longing for respite, he soon headed to Durango, where his uncle helped him find a job doing finish carpentry and set him up in a motel. He managed his speed habit, though he was still smoking hash regularly; and he was able gradually to save some money. He and his uncle made plans to take a camping trip to California once they finished the home they had been working on together. Two weeks into the trip, Jake and his uncle parted their ways after a conflict, and Jake found himself at a crossroads. He didn't have enough money to return to Colorado, and he didn't have a place to stay even if he did. Stuck in Colfax, California, the closest relative he had was the same aunt he had seen at Christmas, who ran an ice cream shop near San Diego. After purchasing a ticket and a pack of cigarettes, he only had five dollars left in his pocket.

He called his mother collect to inform her of his plans, but she discouraged his trip. "My mom told me that my aunt probably didn't want me there," he says. "She had enough to worry about with running her store, and she didn't need some crackhead making things hard." Jake asked his mother to call her sister and tell her that he was coming to San Diego regardless, because he had already bought the ticket with the last of his money. Ten minutes later, his mother called him back and said his aunt not only would help him out, but she considered his arrival to be an answer to prayer.

Jake's aunt arranged a place for him to stay at a nearby ranch with a handful of bikers and ex-convicts who had discovered sobriety. "That night, on the Greyhound bus, somewhere in central California I prayed for the first time in over ten years," he says. The only other time he recalls praying was when he had been in prison. "I don't remember exactly what I said, but it was something along the lines that I could no longer deny that God exists, but I did not know who or what God was. I prayed that if he would reveal himself to me, I would follow and serve him."

Jake got off the bus at six the next morning in San Diego, and his aunt met him with a warm embrace. Three hours later, Jake was in a worship service at his aunt's church. The following day, he started poring over the ads he found for cabinetmakers in the classified ads. Of the thirteen ads in the paper, only one answered his call. The owner, whose shop was less than two miles from where Jake would be staying, offered him work. Without any means of transportation, he borrowed his aunt's bike to get to and from work until he could afford something of his own.

March 8, 2000, was the last day Jake ever did drugs. He went on to become an active member in his aunt's church for several years, studying scripture at every possible opportunity and learning about how to live the faith he claims has saved his life. He met a young woman through a home fellowship group, whom he married on December 7, 2002. He and his wife moved to Denver a few years later, where they are active in a downtown church. Jake is working full-time and is enrolled in an undergraduate program at Colorado Christian University, where he is studying organizational management, with an emphasis on Christian leadership. He hopes to eventually enter into ministry, where he plans to pursue a pastoral position.

Numbers Don't Lie

If one person's story is not enough, consider the following statistics. SAMHSA's National Survey on Drug Use and Health found that 4 million young adults aged eighteen to twenty-five (12.4 percent) used prescription pain relievers (analgesics) such as OxyContin® nonmedically in 2005.[13] Here, we see the obvious signs of a generation in pain. How much clearer must the signs become before we realize a problem exists?

The criminal justice system has been the point of entry for 47 percent of young adults currently in substance abuse treatment, as well as for 52 percent of youths in treatment.[14] Where is the church? Why must we wait for the judicial system to say that these young people need help? Do they have to be arrested in order to receive treatment? Is this the message we send? In a haplessly reactive culture, the church must be a proactive source of hope and healing for these young people, empowering them with the tools they require for self-care before they face these high risk factors. We must also be there for their families, both before and after a crisis is recognized. We should be on the front lines, helping teachers, parents, and other caretakers collectively identify risky and self-destructive behavior before it ever becomes an issue relegated to the court system.

Though it may be the most obvious form of self-destructive behavior, substance abuse is not the only risk factor for young people. Researchers consider gambling to be the fastest growing teenage addiction, with the rate of pathological gambling among high school and college-aged youth to be about twice that of adults. According to Howard J. Shaffer, director of the Harvard Medical School Center for Addiction Studies, "Today, there are more children experiencing adverse symptoms from gambling than from drugs,...and the problem is growing."[15] Imagine the debt incurred at such an early age. Large debt loads can lead to depression, which can lead to other substance abuse later in life as well. Addictions become compounded, as do their impact on individuals and families.

Anorexia affects seven out of every hundred teenage girls, although the illness can be experienced earlier and later in life. Most people who have anorexia are female, but males also develop the disorder. Bulimia may affect up to three in every hundred teenage girls. More females than males also develop bulimia.[16] This means that if you have at least ten youth or young adults in your church, at least one of them probably has an eating disorder. Chances are that as many as half of them are binge drinkers, and one in ten has a very high risk for a long-term struggle with alcoholism and/or gambling.

Again, depression and low self-esteem may lead to more complex addictions and increased stress. The emotional and physical damage comes with a price. Lifelong health problems lead to other challenges for the future.

Some addictions even lead to higher-risk behavior. Consider the following:

> In a sample of college students ages 17 to 24, 47 percent of men and 57 percent of women indicated that they had sexual intercourse one to five times while under the influence of alcohol. Heavy use of alcohol also has been correlated with increased casual sex without condoms and

with increased numbers of sex partners among 18-to-21-year-olds. In a younger teenage sample of 13-to-19-year-olds, respondents admitted engaging in riskier behaviors during sexual encounters when they used alcohol or other substances compared with encounters when they did not use substances.[17]

Interpersonal sexual behavior is only one concern. The advent of the Internet has created both unprecedented accessibility to pornography and anonymity for people of all ages. NetDoctor, an online medical advice service, conducted a survey about online sexual behavior. They found that "a fifth of adults have 'cybered' (had sex to orgasm with someone online)."[18] The survey also found a dramatic rise in sexually addictive behavior both among adults and teenagers. "There's nothing new in 14-year-old boys looking at porn," says the report. "What is different is the range, volume and accessibility of sexual material that technology allows."[19]

Not only do young people's addictions need to be recognized, but they also need to be acknowledged for the painful realities they create and the damage they cause in all lives. Ignoring them is not the social equivalent of turning the other cheek. In not taking action, we are turning our heads away.

God of Rock

From the legends about blues musicians selling their souls at the crossroads to Elvis's gyrating hips, rock music has generally been seen as synonymous with a countercultural movement. However, in the past three decades, a radical change has taken place in the Christian approach to praise and worship music. What once was a small murmur from the fringes of the folk music era in the 1970s has now become a multimillion-dollar industry. Contemporary Christian music has transformed Christian worship in millions of churches worldwide. Embraced by many and shunned both by some religious and musical purists, contemporary Christian music can be a divisive, and even grossly misunderstood, phenomenon.

Although the movement is relatively new, its origins can be traced all the way back to Martin Luther, who called for art, and particularly music, to be used in as many ways as possible to glorify God. In this chapter, we recognize some of the messages contained in contemporary music, as well as findings from our research about young adults and their preference for music in worship. While many may believe that all young adults prefer the new over the old, this assumption may be a dangerously broad generalization that, in the spirit of Martin Luther, may reject more than is necessary in its effort to establish a unique identity apart from established traditions.

Fair to Compare?

Can one reasonably compare sacred music with so-called secular music? Is there a clear–or even necessary–distinction between worship music and other music? What is the purpose of music in a worship setting, and are there right and wrong ways to approach it? Such questions, and the answers to them, help us better understand the value we place on this highly expressive and deeply personal art form, which has become central to most worship experiences.

As consolation to those who have less than a firm grasp on the place of music in the faith experience, those who compose, perform, and market sacred music have strong and widely varying opinions within the industry too. In an October 2004 article on the Surefish Web site,[1] Lev Eakins discusses Christian music with both participants and fans at the Greenbelt Christian Arts and Music Festival. From these conversations, he developed several categories of thought surrounding the role and identity of sacred music:

Purist: This school of thought suggests that music should be used solely to glorify God. This position adheres most strictly to Luther's teaching, drawing a distinct line between sacred and secular music. To achieve this, musicians must always stay completely focused on their evangelical mission, rather than the trappings of fame and adulation that may accompany this line of work. Likewise, fans must stay centered on the Christian message, rather than the artists themselves or on the music as entertainment.

Spiritually Reflective: This camp recognizes not only the theological merit of music, but also its ability to inspire and the artistic integrity of the art form itself. For these artists, spirituality is central to their art but is not the exclusive driving force behind everything they create. Those who consider themselves to take a more spiritually reflective approach to music sometimes criticize contemporary Christian music as a genre for its lack of quality or originality, claiming it often sacrifices musical integrity in an effort to adhere to its message.

Incidentalist: Incidentalists do not particularly care what the original intent of the artist was in creating the music. If someone finds inspiration in it, that is all that matters. This mind-set does not limit the music that can be inspiring to self-avowed "Christian" artists, but rather says that inspiration can come from artists of all backgrounds or even no faith background. In this case, the inspiration may come form the message itself, or it may be a more aesthetic experience of beauty, inclining the mind and spirit toward God.

Separatist: This most fundamental, absolute mind-set asserts that rock music, or contemporary music as a whole for that matter, has no place in worship and in the Christian culture. This mind-set adheres more to the original experience of rock and roll by its detractors, who believed that such music was of the devil and not to be embraced in any form by faithful Christians.

Surprisingly, when asked if Christian music in general is as good as secular popular music, most Christian musicians at the festival quickly replied with a resounding no. This, however, is a highly subjective and inexact generalization, as no established criteria exist to compare the relative quality of sacred music to the work of other artists. However, it is not insignificant that many of the artists who write and perform the music readily concede that their genre of music is inferior.

Eakins also noted that most artists with whom he spoke at the festival identified most closely with the spiritually reflective or incidental approaches. Even those who write and perform sacred music for a living felt it was not necessary to draw lines between one type of music and another. However, a clear market exists for what they do, and plenty of musicians and recording companies are willing to help fill this need.

More record executives than artists fall within the purist or separatist camps. Whether this is a matter of ideology or brand identity is unclear, but those who control the production and distribution of the content ultimately maintain disproportionate control over what the artists are allowed to present to the public. Record company control occurs in the secular music industry as well. For several years in college and immediately following, Christian worked for a number of major record companies. While a few multiplatinum-caliber artists had earned the latitude to express themselves as they wished, others were kept on a short leash. Though a more altruistic mission than their secular counterparts may drive producers of sacred music, the bottom line is undeniable. Record companies must meet certain sales thresholds or they will go out of business, regardless of the message the music conveys.

How is it possible to have such a disconnection between consumers, artists, and music executives in the sacred music community? Further, what possible negative effect does such a genre of music have on peoples' perception of Christianity if so many fans and artists even within the community acknowledge the quality is not as good? We consider this and the responses we received on our survey about preferred music styles in the final part of this chapter. First, Christian shares his faith story, as well as the role music plays for him as a worship leader, an artist, and as a person of faith.

Christian's Story

As is typical of many people in my generation, I know relatively little about my family and cultural history. I know I have some Scottish, Welsh, and Irish blood, and that my last name is adapted from the French name Pyeatt. On my mother's side, I have been told that we are descendants of the Lilly family, the founders of the Lilly pharmaceutical empire. This ancestry might mean more for me, but about five generations back, my great-great-great-grandfather married a full-blooded Cherokee woman. This prompted the Lilly family to disown him and hence sever my claim to the Lilly fortune.

My dad's side has few stories to share as well. My grandfather was a dark, complicated person. Though unusually intelligent, he also suffered from deep depression, medicating himself daily with alcohol. As a child, he found his mother in the garage of their home after she had shot herself in the head. This incident, combined with being raised by a fiercely strict and equally angry father, likely contributed to his own grim disposition.

My parents, Frank and Linda, met in July of 1966. They had their first date in November of that same year and got engaged on December 2, during their second date. They were married on April 1, 1967; she was nineteen and he was twenty. Frank attended a few services at the Baptist church where Linda played piano for the youth choir during their engagement. A few weeks before the wedding, a traveling evangelist visited the church for a revival. The minister was fiery in his rhetoric, raining images of end-times and brimstone down upon the daunted congregation.

Shaken and disheartened by the experience, Frank reconsidered his commitment to the church. He explained to Linda that he could not, in good conscience, be a part of a faith community that supported such ideas. He offered her a way out, saying that he would understand if this meant she could not marry him. At the time, all she could think about was that the invitations to the wedding were already in the mail. Facing a potential crisis, she opted to stay the course and go through with the ceremony.

I was born at Baylor Hospital in downtown Dallas on October 7, 1971. I am the only male still carrying on the Piatt name, as has been the pattern for at least half a dozen generations or more. More than a hundred years ago, however, our bloodline actually was sired by a neighbor, because my great-great-great-grandfather–give or take a generation–was sterile.

My grandmother, Betty Piatt, whom we called Pi, came to town to celebrate my arrival. Being a lifelong Episcopalian, she saw great value in the christening ritual performed with infants. Though neither of my parents had any affiliation with the Episcopal Church at the time, they had me christened at the Church of the Incarnation, largely to humor Pi. I was eight-days-old.

I was named Christian, which of course means "follower of Christ." I've also heard the term "little Christ" used to define the name, though neither comes without a significant amount of spiritual weight. My middle name, Damien, came from the name of the priest who was the protagonist in William Peter Blatty's book, *The Exorcist*. My mom was reading this book while pregnant with me, and she liked the sound of it. With a little research, she learned the name meant "faithful follower," which fit well with the first name already selected for me.

Several years later the cult film classic *The Omen* would wreak havoc with the name Damien, the moniker borne in the movie by the fiendish young spawn of Satan. I have never been able to shake peoples' perception that the name is somehow inherently evil ever since, though an explanation of the true origin of my middle name doesn't sway them in a new direction.

My given names suggest I was destined from birth to follow *something*. Being the only child of two parents who worked through most of my childhood, I became relatively self-sufficient out of necessity, and my own introverted disposition made me even less of the following type. I was a decent student and did well enough through my middle school years, until I developed a more fierce sense of autonomy during adolescence. Even then, I was restless about matters of faith, purpose, and justice. However, rather than following the words or deeds of my peers or potential mentors, I turned increasingly inward, cultivating an inner voice and sense of calling. Though this worked in some cases, it was also a key contributor to many of the 'desert times' that followed over the next decade or more.

My earliest memories of church began around 1974, when I attended preschool at First Baptist in Garland, Texas. I had a friend, Edward, who resolved to help me dig our way to China by way of the sandbox. Enormous sycamore trees surrounded the church, and we walked through them as we learned the story of Zacchaeus. It was a loving, safe place where I found many friends among the children and teachers. I attended Sunday services with my mom, who cut puzzles out of the weekend paper, pasting them into a notebook to which I only had access during church. I vividly remember my ears tingling whenever the pastor would say the word *Christian*, assuming I was being addressed personally.

As I grew older, my mom gave me lists of Bible verses to look up, keeping me occupied long enough to endure the sermon. Between this and being raised in a Baptist preschool, I got to know scripture fairly well at an early age. Every Sunday morning before church, my mom took me to the Southern Maid donut shop for donut holes and chocolate milk. This, combined with the allure of time alone with my mom, was enough to get me out of bed almost every week. I don't remember my dad ever joining us, which I found curious as well as completely natural. Neither parent forced me to align with their respective views. I always knew my attendance at church was voluntary.

We moved north to Carrollton, a suburb of Dallas, so my dad could relocate to a promising new insurance office, surrounded by new development. My mom and I visited a few churches, but never found a place to call home. Then a local pastor came to our door and invited us to visit his new church. The Baptist church had begun as a study group in the living room of one of the founding members, and now the church was going to begin meeting in the cafeteria at a local elementary school. The group was warm and energized by the possibilities of a new church, and we soon joined on a permanent basis.

As is common with small churches, we got plugged in to any number of "opportunities for ministry" from day one. Within weeks, my mom was playing piano regularly, and not long after she became my Sunday school teacher. We practiced memorizing Bible verses and discussed the typical stories shared in most children's church settings.

In fifth grade, I transferred from Greenhill, a private college preparatory school, to St. Mark's, an all-boys prep academy. Though St. Mark's was no longer affiliated with the Protestant leadership that had founded the school, I attended chapel twice a week and completed requisite religion classes, which were unapologetically Christian in emphasis. Ironically, here I encountered my first experience with Jewish culture, because nearly a third of the student body was Jewish. To them, the caliber of education overrode any ideological differences presented by the religious slant of the program. At St. Mark's I began to understand that the rest of the world did not necessarily share my particular understanding of faith.

I had the privilege of sharing in a number of Hanukah celebrations with some of my friends, and at age thirteen, I joined the rest of the student body in making the rounds to more than a dozen Bar Mitzvahs. I took part in my first Passover Seder, a fascinating ritual feast, complete with Hebrew prayers and traditional foods. The interfaith experiences only whetted my thirst for a broader spiritual understanding. What more, I thought, must be out there? How much bigger might God be than I pictured in the felt-board stories of the Sunday school room?

A student at Dallas Theological Seminary, arguably the most conservative theological school in the area, became our youth group leader. In part this was because of his enthusiasm for youth ministry, and also because his wife agreed to team teach with him. Though I liked him very much as a person, we were on different spiritual paths. For example, though I learned about the theory of evolution in school, on Sundays he explained that scientists fabricated the fossil record and that dinosaurs never existed. He believed God created the world in six days. When I asked him how a day could even exist before the earth was set in motion around the sun, arguments about semantics and the shaky foundation of my faith ensued. I was attending a school rich with interfaith culture, which fostered independent and critical thought, and increasingly I found the didactic lectures of the youth group stifling, if not deluded.

My contention was that God gave me a brain to use and that blind acceptance was spiritually shallow. While my youth group leader was eager to share his understanding of scripture, he was less eager to engage an uppity teenager about why he questioned what he was taught. Faith, after all, was imparted, not wrestled with. My questions, then, stemmed from a fundamental rejection of the principles I was taught. I refused to accept that my devoutly Jewish friends were condemned to hell, simply because they weren't raised in the same faith tradition as I was. I started to wonder if a theological system that rejected people I cared about, including my own father, was appropriate for me.

By that time, the youth ministry couple had moved on, and another couple took their place. Again, I cared deeply for them both as people, and their hearts were truly invested in my spiritual welfare.

Unfortunately, ideology trumped personal bonds once again, and I found myself outside the circle of acceptable belief. My decision to leave the church culminated during a particularly heated discussion about the book of Revelation, during which I questioned the literal depictions of horses descending from the clouds and fantastic beasts exacting terror upon the barren landscape.

"If you can't just believe what the Bible says," fumed the youth leader, "then it doesn't mean shit to you!" He punctuated his point by hurling the Good Book at my head, barely missing me.

We all agreed it was best for me to seek my spiritual nourishment elsewhere. I was seventeen. Within a year, halfway through my senior year in high school, my parents got divorced. I was old enough at that point to choose where I would live, so I moved out of our expansive home and into a cramped townhome with my mom.

Our oversized, elegant furniture seemed out of place in the modest rooms, but we made the place a home for the months leading up to my departure for college. By that time, my mom had enough of her own issues without having to play parent to me, and I was more than ready to stretch my independence. We were more like roommates than family. Though I was grateful for the latitude, a part of me still longed for the idyllic family I would never have. My parents, set adrift to rediscover themselves as single adults, joined me in my restlessness.

I steered clear of religion for some time, not revisiting my faith until college. I visited a few churches, from Episcopal to Unitarian, but I failed to find a context within which I could engage theological questions in the ways I sought. Not until I took several philosophy classes about metaphysics and Asian religions did my peripheral vision expand once again in a way that touched something meaningful. I found an exhilarating synergy between the Buddhist philosophies I read about and the teachings of Jesus. Soon, I became convinced that Jesus likely studied Buddhism during the so-called "missing years" of his life, from age twelve until he began his ministry at thirty. If Jesus had these missing years, why couldn't I? I gave myself permission to explore everything from Hinduism's Baghavad Gita to the I Ching, Aristotle, and Heidegger.

I read obsessively, connecting with Robert Pirsig's *Zen and the Art of Motorcycle Maintenance* and Nikos Kazantzakis's *The Last Temptation of Christ*. I melded together a hodgepodge of religion, philosophy, and popular culture into a worldview that was uniquely my own. Though I felt some satisfaction with the freedom I had afforded myself to stretch my own understanding of God, I was increasingly spiritually isolated. I spoke less and less about my own beliefs, assuming my ideas were too idiosyncratic, if not heretical, for anyone else to accept. For ten years, I abandoned the possibility of a corporate theological experience, in exchange for a custom-tailored understanding of the Divine.

I wasn't reclusive in all areas of my life, just my religious practice. My primary social outlet was music. I had played drums since fifth grade, but in high school I figured out three things. First, singing and playing guitar was a better way for me to express myself creatively. Second, a guitar was much more portable and convenient than hauling a drum set everywhere. Finally, and perhaps most important, I realized that chicks loved singers. I was sold.

I played solo shows around Dallas in high school, and in college, I graduated to being the front man in a few rock bands. This experience was the key to my college social life. From fraternity parties to nightclubs, my friends and I made it our goal to play somewhere every weekend. In some ways, it was one of the most exciting times of my life. However, given the venues where we played and some of the crowds I hung out with, I considered my music completely divorced from my spiritual life.

In 1998, I met Amy, the woman who would become my wife, on a blind date. I worked with her aunt in Pueblo, Colorado, where I was an educational consultant. I was just bored and lonely enough to drive 110 miles north to go out to dinner with a woman I had never met. Though I doubted my own judgment all the way to Denver, I reflect upon that risk as one of the smartest I have taken in my life.

In part, the relationship worked because, ironically, neither of us was looking for a relationship. Amy had just ended a long-term romance, and I was scheduled to move to Seattle within two months. But what should have been a convenient diversion became an undeniable bond. We carried on our relationship long-distance from Denver to Seattle for close to a year, until I had the chance to return to Colorado for work. Within six more months, we were engaged. We were married in Amy's father's church on July 15, 2000.

Amy also was involved in ministry, which presented a challenge for me at first. I was hesitant to jump back into any organized religion, as I had been exploring on my own for about a decade. She was serving as the associate pastor at a small young adult church when I met her. She invited me every week to their casual, Sunday evening services, and I politely declined for several weeks. It became clear, however, that this would either become something that drew us together or a wedge that finally sent us our separate ways. I had fallen for her so quickly and completely that I resolved to put my own defenses aside and visit the church.

I found the group of twenty or so worshipers to be unassuming, anything but judgmental and, to my relief, more interested in me as a person than as a soul that needed saving. I also knew they looked to Amy as an example of spirituality, as did I, which afforded us some common ground from day one. They sat in the round, and everyone took part in the service. If not for the message delivered by the minister, one could hardly have separated the leadership from the congregation. It was just a group who came together to sing, study, and talk about their faith. They went around the corner after services to a cool restaurant and invited me along. Many of my reservations waned, though I still waited in the back of my mind for the trap I figured had to be coming.

But they had no other agenda. What I brought to the church was enough, and in fact, they appreciated my differences, which was thoroughly novel in my experience with church. One week the minister asked me if I would bring my guitar and sing the following Sunday during church. I balked, explaining that I didn't know any "church" music. He shrugged and said that wasn't necessarily what he had in mind. He asked me instead to share something meaningful to me, something that came from my heart. Anxiously, I agreed.

The next week, I had two songs of my own I planned to share during communion and a special time of meditation. I had hardly made my way through the first chorus, however, before I felt a lump rising in my throat. My voice wavered, but I persisted until I reached the end of the song, at which point the dam broke and I dissolved into sobs of release. The other worshipers hardly knew what to make of my theatrics, but they smiled and just let me cry. In offering up that one song in God's presence, more than a decade of pain, resistance, and longing fell away, much to my surprise.

I collected myself just enough to play through the next song a few minutes later, followed by more bawling. They were the least painful tears I had shed in my life. I felt as if I was laying down a weight I had carried on my own for much of my life. I can't explain the experience as anything other than a holy moment. The music opened me up before everyone, letting in just enough light to warm the remotest parts of me I usually kept to myself.

The minister asked Amy and me to sing "Amazing Grace" at his wedding the following summer, shortly after I returned from Seattle. We sang a cappella from the rear balcony of the church, invisible to the rest of the congregation. After the service, he thanked us for our offering and introduced me to a friend of his from seminary, who was leading a small congregation in Texas.

"What I wouldn't give for someone like you to lead worship for us in Texas," he said, smiling. "Too bad you live all the way up here. It would be a heck of a commute." What he didn't know at the time was that Amy had just accepted a scholarship at a seminary in the same city the week before. When I shared this with him, he could not stand still. He wore his elation all over his face, a trait I came to love dearly about him. I tried to qualify this bit of providence with an explanation about how I knew nothing about worship music, let alone leading services.

"I'm not really into Michael W. Smith and the whole Christian music thing," I explained.

"Perfect," he said, "neither am I."

I became the music minister at the small Disciples of Christ church in Texas within weeks of moving there for Amy's graduate school. It was like no other church I had seen before. Those who came were committed to social justice not only in word, but in deed as well. Immediately, I felt a kinship there that would last for some time.

As my confidence grew, I began to preach on occasion, and after about a year, I started a new midweek young adult worship service called Inner Mission. The pulpit was filled by new seminary students every week, eager to practice their preaching skills. The group was small but sincere, and I learned through that experience that I had a calling to leadership within the church. By then, Amy had accepted a position as the associate minister there, and for the first time, we worked together in team ministry.

As intense and fulfilling as our positive experiences were, the dark times were equally heartbreaking. Amy ended up filing sexual misconduct charges with the region against the senior minister, and within days, the entire church turned away from us. We received angry calls late at night, and rumors spread like a virus across the seminary campus. By order of the region, however, we could not speak about the proceedings as they investigated the charges, which only angered the members of the church even more. They could not understand why we went to the region rather than coming to the church with our concerns. Aside from the region's protocol in handling the issues, we faced the matter of the accused person's relationship to the leadership. His parents, as well as his sister, were all part of the church's board.

We had decided the only way to address the problem was to reach beyond the boundaries of the congregation, which was interpreted by those on the inside as abject betrayal. Though I understood their reaction on some level, the feeling of alienation contrasted starkly against the apparent blind fidelity they showed for this man who was the subject of the investigation. We had lost a faith family overnight, on top of the experiences that precipitated the investigation in the first place. Not being able to talk about the situation with anyone only made things worse.

After what seemed like an eternity, disciplinary actions were taken against him, and we tried to put the experience behind us. Amy took a position as an associate minister at another church, and I resolved to take a sabbatical from my heavy involvement. I still went to services, but the trauma of my previous experience gave me just cause for erecting some of the boundaries I had eagerly let down before. Our new congregation was caring and nurturing, but I had little to offer them in return.

New hope entered my life during that time in the form of a son. The combination of utter vulnerability, joy, and fullness accompanied little Mattias's arrival. In his face, I saw God, as he squirmed constantly in my trembling arms. Love was made flesh in that moment, and another dimension was added to my understanding of the Christian story, manifested in the birth of a similarly helpless child, two thousand years earlier.

After three and a half years of study, Amy completed her time at seminary, and we began our search for a place to serve. Though the prospect of starting a new church was intimidating, we both felt drawn in that direction. Amy found an ad for a new church in the back of *DisciplesWorld* magazine that hooked us both immediately. The new church team sought to plant a church that would "give itself away to the community," a mission with which we readily resonated. Only after investigating further did we learn the church was to be located in Pueblo, Colorado, Amy's hometown and the place I had been working when I first met her.

We packed our belongings in a van early in the summer of 2004 and headed west. We began Milagro Christian Church, which is Spanish for "miracle," in our living room. After several months, we moved into a space at the local university, and then into an old church on the south side of town, where we serve today. We are now in our third year, and we see our ministry as a team effort, though Amy is the only paid staff person. Now Milagro faces the same questions with which any new church must contend, including the nature of our ministry and the needs we will meet as a family of faith.

My primary responsibility at Milagro is to lead worship through music. Following the much-needed break, I am enjoying new life as an active participant in others' worship experience through the musical medium. We are intentional about as much as possible, from the placement of the musicians in the worship space to the songs we select for each service. For most in the congregation, the music team is practically invisible. We have a stage in front, though we set up off to the side. We focus as much as possible on the use of acoustic instruments, as they have a more timeless attraction about them that feels more personal. We employ a broad range of musical styles from popular secular songs to old gospel hymns, but if done correctly, each piece is part of a greater trajectory, leading us as a body of worshipers toward a mutually desirable destination.

I can never tell what music will connect with whom, so I have given up trying to guess. What I do notice, however, is that the simplest songs often have the most profound impact. We insert intentional periods of silence, as well as a capella pieces and simple refrains whenever possible, as they draw people in rather than forcing them into a more passive "receive" mode. We are sensitive about the use of God imagery in our music, and any potential sense of exclusion a song might communicate to those who are worshiping with us. We do not avoid all male God language, but we also enjoy feminine perspectives of the divine.

The highest compliment I can receive as a worship leader is that someone sensed a spirit of true worship. I prefer this to accolades for a particular song or solo. In the end, music and other media should move the corporate experience forward. When I am engaged in leading worship, I am either working toward that goal or fighting against it, and knowing which is taking place at any given time is difficult to discern until you are in the middle of one of those spontaneously sacred moments, when you look around, pause, and say, "Yes, certainly God is with us in this place."

A Window to the Divine

For me, music always has been the most concrete manifestation of divine inspiration. From the first time I heard Mozart's *Requiem* to the heavy metal concerts of my high school days, music has moved me in profound and inexplicable ways. As noted in my story above, I saw sacred and secular music as necessarily distinct throughout my childhood, but my own "worldly" music actually helped reintroduce me to my deep need for a shared faith experience.

Though I grew up with a more implicitly purist understanding of worship music, I have since gravitated toward a combination of the spiritually reflective and incidental schools of thought. Part of my familial, and even cultural, heritage lies in the roots of southern gospel music. Four generations back, and perhaps earlier, my mother's family gathered before a neighbor's barn on the weekends to play hymns together. My grandmother played guitar and sang while my great-grandmother played piano. For them, those sacred songs were a bond of blood, spirit, and heart. The moments they shared after a week of backbreaking work in the peanut fields of West Texas were sacred. Together, they worshiped, though not in a church, and they celebrated, though without benefit of a minister, liturgy, or the vestments of an otherwise sacred setting.

Many of the songs they sang together were the same as those in church, and in carrying those songs with them throughout the week, they also brought a sense of worshipfulness with them. I've heard stories about my grandparents singing "In the Sweet By and By" and "What a Friend We Have in Jesus" as they shook peanuts, row after row. The music not only became a component of their Sunday service, but it became a metaphor for their rural culture and shared experience. It connected them to something greater than themselves, their hunger pangs, blistered hands, and sunburned shoulders.

Put simply, the music inspired them.

For me, these songs represent something greater as well. I grew up with very little sense of connection to any cultural or familial identity beyond the two generations directly involved in my upbringing. Many of the songs shared with me reach back more than a century and have been sung by millions of people in numerous styles. In bringing them to life at home and at church, I immediately connect with a rich, beautiful musical heritage with which I can identify. This connection helps place me much more easily into a state of mind to receive inspiration and to share in a sacred moment with those around me.

Our church combines a wide array of musical styles in our worship environment. We include everything from secular rock music to ancient folk songs and from traditional hymns to contemporary praise music, depending on the message we are trying to convey. However, the most universally embraced songs seem to be those from my southern gospel roots. Perhaps I bring a special spiritual fervor to these songs as the worship leader, or maybe people of all ages come to church, longing to be inspired and to feel connected to something greater than the world they see during the rest of the week.

Each person generally connects with something different in each worship service; however, the oldest traditional gospel hymns possess a unique resonance across generations. We employ many of the instruments from my family's tradition as well, including upright bass, mandolin, acoustic guitar, piano, and even banjo. The resurgence of bluegrass and acoustic music in the past several years has also helped open people's minds and ears to this tradition. The lyrics are often poetic and carefully crafted, with solid biblical foundations and with deeply unique roots in American culture.

Regarding secular music, we are careful about how and why we use songs not originally intended for a worship setting. I visited an enormous church in Texas a few years ago, complete with plasma screens, canister lights, and all of the other technological components generally associated with a rock concert. As I entered, the band broke into "Don't Know Why" by Norah Jones, followed by Bon Jovi's "Livin' on a Prayer." Though the second song does have the word *prayer* in the chorus, I was never able to make the connection between this song and the theme of the worship, and I found no sacred connection with the Norah Jones song whatsoever. The music was professionally performed, however, and the crowd of several thousand received it eagerly. I just could not get past the lingering sense that I was being entertained rather than being led in worship.

Having said this, I do use a number of songs by secular artists at times in our church, including "Still Haven't Found What I'm

Looking For" by U2, "I Will Remember You" by Sarah McLachlan, "With My Own Two Hands" by Ben Harper and Jack Johnson, and "One Love" by Bob Marley. When employed, such songs can guide people toward a new level of awareness about the message of the song they may have heard in another context for many years, imbuing it with new relevance. Time and again, I've had people tell me after a service when one of these songs was used that they appreciated hearing these familiar songs in new ways, and that by connecting to something familiar to them in the "real world," they found themselves more open to the message of the service. I don't ever use a secular song in worship, though, without asking myself what ultimate purpose the piece is to serve.

For the most part, young adults are receptive to alternative media introduced into a church setting, such as secular music, movies, books, or television shows. In our young adult survey, only 13 percent of those respondents said they felt the use of secular media in church was not appropriate, while two thirds agreed that the use of such media is acceptable. One of the misconceptions about young adults, however, is that they all prefer contemporary praise music in church.

In our survey, we listed twelve different styles of music and allowed people to mark all those they preferred in worship. Though the most popular response was "Contemporary Praise" with 234 responses, and "Hymns with Piano" was close behind with 228 responses, followed by "Blended" style (a combination of contemporary and traditional music) with 221. "Hymns with Organ," "Choral Music," and "A Capella" musical styles were also highly popular, with 179, 177, and 172 responses, respectively.

I must admit my own personal bias against much of the contemporary praise music I have encountered. For one, I resonate with the majority of young people who spoke with Lev Eakins for his Surefish article. In my experience, contemporary worship music generally isn't as well performed or composed as mainstream secular music, and much of it is homogenously arranged the same way over and over again. It sounds as if someone handed out a rule book to contemporary Christian musicians, dictating that all worship music must contain an airy keyboard part and breathy vocals.

Granted, the last few years have given rise to a much broader diversity of sacred music, from hardcore metal to rap and punk. However, a common thread remains among much of contemporary worship lyrics that some struggle with at best. At worst, they find it alienating. Much of the language of contemporary worship music is surprisingly antiquated, harkening back to seventeenth-century images of kings, thrones, and royal courts. Though this type of verbiage is employed throughout the *King James Version of the Bible,* many versions preferred by young adults, such as the *New International Version* (NIV), the *New Revised Standard Version* (NRSV) and interpretations such as *The Message,* have departed from this sort of "feudal" language.

While some may argue that this sort of language is more scripturally faithful, it fails to bridge a cultural chasm for those less familiar with biblical texts. Also, too often contemporary music focuses on the praise component of the faith experience, while minimizing or completely ignoring the many other dimensions of spiritual life. Granted, praise is important, especially in worship. However, for someone unsure of what they believe or for someone facing a situation that challenges their faith, such as addiction, death, or other crises, such positively skewed themes may actually cause them to feel they are failing in their faith if they aren't happy all of the time.

Great art reflects the many vicissitudes of daily life, rich with beauty, tragedy, mystery, and mourning. Insofar as worship music, or worship as a whole, reflects only affirmative faith experiences, it renders itself one-dimensional, and for those who do not claim a like faith, potentially irrelevant or trite. Perhaps the greatest issue with worship music is not its inherent quality, but its overall significance to the human experience. Churches are best served by asking themselves what they hope to achieve with their music programs, and whether or not their offerings reflect the reality of either the people in attendance or, taken one step further, the reality of those they hope to attract. To assume an entire generation is drawn toward one particular type of music is to feed into the sense that many young adults have about the church being out of touch, disconnected, and even indifferent to the needs and values of the world around it.

Finally, I'd like to comment on the use of technology along with worship music, as this is an increasingly popular trend. We use a digital projector and computer-generated slide show in most of our services in a number of ways. First, because we do not use songs that are generally contained within a single songbook, it keeps us from having to waste paper by printing out individual songsheets every week. Also, we find that the screen tends to make people look up, whereas hymnals and songsheets cause them to look down toward their laps. In this sense, technology helps facilitate a more communal worship experience.

Amy also appreciates the ability to share vivid illustrations of her sermon points on occasion. The saying that a picture says a thousand words is not without some truth, though misplaced or superfluous imagery can prove more distracting than helpful. Fred Craddock suggests that we ask ourselves what effect the media we employ in worship has on the one experiencing it. Does it draw them in, or does it cause them to lean back? In a culture where we have become relatively passive filters of an increasingly overwhelming volume of data, the church should have anything but the same "lean-back" effect as the rest of daily life tends to have.

Keeping in mind that music and art ideally stimulate the imagination, we must be mindful to leave time and space for the imagination to operate. In some cases, a particular image, video, or sound clip may provoke emotional responses or lead to engaging dialogue. Too often, media in church begins to reflect the rapid-fire flood of sensory input to which we can so easily become inured. Its purpose is reduced to yet another distraction or so much superficial entertainment without a significant lingering effect. A reasonable rule of thumb is to ask yourself: "Is this a component of worship that I can't express any other way?" or "Is the potential impact of this piece of media profound enough to stick with people all week long?"

If the answer to either of these questions is not a confident yes, you may want to reconsider its value to the overall worship experience. We must also be aware of what may come across as exclusive, as opposed to inclusive, in our music and media selections. We can easily pick a song for worship because a certain key word fits with the overall theme or simply because we like the mood it sets. However, we must assume that someone who has never been to church will be worshiping with us in any given week. How might they receive the message we're communicating? Does it welcome them to explore deep spiritual questions alongside us, or does it convey an assumed internal knowledge, held only by those already part of the faith community?

Sometimes we approach worship as if it's something we're doing only because the invitations have already been sent out. People expect us to be there, and they expect certain traditions, prayers, or even songs to be done, simply because it's what they are accustomed to. Our responsibility, however, as leaders in worship for persons at all points along their own spiritual path, is to inspire, enliven, renew, and sometimes challenge. We're not responsible for making people comfortable, for keeping them happy, or for simply reinforcing what they already believe.

We are bound by a covenant of spiritual leadership to walk alongside our brothers and sisters of faith, to bring hope to a suffering world, and to manifest the light of creation that burns within us. Music is one of the most unique and beautiful creations in the history of the world. If it is reduced to anything less than a connection to God's inspired creation, we run the risk of straying from our call to lead people toward a full and life-giving experience of God.

Who May Serve?

By the year 2025, approximately five out of every six current clergy leaders will retire. With an average age in the mid to late thirties for seminary graduates, the average tenure of a clergy person is at least a decade less than in other first career professions.[1] Aside from these age and attrition issues, representation within church leadership is also an issue. Though most churches are experiencing the greatest growth in membership within non-Anglo ethnicities, a significant majority of church leadership is still white. Though a majority of those who attend church are female, most clergy are male. Such gender, age, and ethnicity gaps help to further reinforce the sense that churches are decreasingly relevant with respect to real-world issues. Meanwhile, churches face a looming vacuum in the pulpit, which may or may not be able to be filled with willing and qualified candidates.

The Web site for Louisville Presbyterian Theological Seminary offers some thoughts on trends within their church leadership:

- The current demand for youth ministry will escalate dramatically. Today there is an acute shortage of youth ministers, in part because ministers as a group are older. The average age of a seminarian today is approximately 33; after three years of study, few of these students in their late 30s or 40s are interested in ministry with junior and senior high youth.
- On the other hand, if there is leadership and vision in congregations, denominations, and seminaries, there is an expanding pool of young people who can be and should be inspired with the challenges and opportunities for a vocation within the church.

• For denominations such as the Presbyterian Church (USA), which is 95% Caucasian, there is an urgent need to recognize the ethnic diversity of young people today and attract them into the life of the church and its leadership. This is not only practical and common sense, it is also a faithful response to the call of Christ to people of all nations and a realization of Peter's dream of the sheet descending from heaven (Acts 10).[2]

Seminary Trends

We find some promising developments in the makeup of those entering into ministry training. In the past four decades, the number of students enrolled in America's Protestant, Roman Catholic, and Greek Orthodox seminaries has grown from 25,000 to 65,000 students, though more than half of these are older than thirty-five when they begin their theological education.[3] The makeup of seminary student bodies is increasingly reflective of the world around them, with respect to gender and ethnicity. In addition, the curricula of these ministry programs are sensitive to the need to prepare tomorrow's church leaders for a different world.

Jules Glanzer, dean of George Fox Seminary, cites the need for such schools to be proactive about matters that will face their students upon graduation. "The society in which our students serve is culturally diverse, postmodern, and post-denominational," says Glanzer. "The faculty understands this context and prepares students for effective ministry in a diverse world. Students are encouraged to confront and address the pressing issues of our world and to meet societal and personal needs in a responsively creative and culturally relevant way."[4]

Relevant curriculum and a diverse body of seminary students are only two of the concerns to be considered, however. William Willimon, former dean of the chapel at Duke University and one of the United Methodist Church's most renowned preachers, decries the quality of students entering many seminaries today. "While about 10% of his seminary students are exceptional, and about 50% of his students have potential that the seminary has an obligation to develop, the remainder are mediocre. They seem to be more interested in the secure living offered by the clergy than they are in finding and fulfilling God's call and pursuing excellence in ministry.

This malaise among clergy is responsible for the UMC's [United Methodist Church's] loss of 2 million members within the past 20 years."[5]

Not all within the greater Christian church believe that the broadening of the scope of seminaries and who they attract and train for ministry has a positive effect on the institution of church and society as a whole. George Neumayr, once a media fellow at the Hoover Institution, notes the following in a March 2002 article, posted on the American Prowler Web site:

> After Vatican II the American Catholic Church very stupidly took the advice of the secular culture and adopted a permissive attitude. 'Loosen up,' 'Don't be judgmental,' 'Accept nontraditional types into the priesthood,' is what the secular culture outside and inside the Church told the American bishops—and they did. Seminaries soon became havens for sexual oddballs. True, the introduction of moral liberalism into the American Catholic Church is not the only cause of the pedophilia problem in the Church. Man's power to choose evil freely is the primary explanation for scandal. But moral liberalism—which tends to rationalize and even sanctify the effects of original sin—abets the spread of sexual sin in the Church.[6]

Other Christian leaders believe that the historical restrictiveness of the church has created the divisions, animosity, mistrust, and abuse we now seek to reconcile. In an August 1994 letter to members of the Episcopal House of Bishops, and hence to the church at large, Rev. John Shelby Spong, retired bishop of the Episcopal Diocese of Newark, New Jersey, claimed that, "some members of our church no longer feel included, where those living in non-traditional relationships might no longer expect to find a place or a welcome in the Body of Christ and where gay and lesbian clergy might question whether or not their gifts are still wanted by the church they love."[7]

Spong notes that as much as one third of the populations in major urban settings identify themselves as gay or lesbian. Spong claims that by allowing ministers to live as openly gay or lesbian and by encouraging them to model committed, loving relationships with their partners, these church leaders bring, "both the hope and love of Christ to communities of people long oppressed, long denigrated, and long judged by various religious authorities as inadequate human beings in whom the image of God is somehow flawed."[8]

The Great Divide

We are witnessing a division within the greater church. As ministry gradually begins to reflect the greater pluralism of the American culture around it, inevitable impasses arise with respect to traditional values, morals, and guidelines about who may and may not serve as leaders. While in some cases we have moved assertively toward a more diverse body of church leadership, others resist such change. Examples of more progressive steps include the election of Sharon Watkins, the first female general minister and president of the Christian Church (Disciples of Christ), the selection of Katharine Jefferts Schori to lead the American Episcopal Church, and the consecration of Gene Robinson, the Episcopal bishop of New Hampshire who is openly gay.

Though generally not as inflammatory as matters of sexuality, gender issues still pose a major point of potential division. The Southern Baptist Convention still claims women should not be allowed to preach or lead churches, based upon a verse in 1 Timothy, wherein Paul says, "I permit no woman to teach or to have authority over a man; she is to keep silent (1 Tim. 2:12). The issue entered the media spotlight in January 2007, when Dr. Sheri Klouda, professor of theology at Southwest Theological Seminary since 2002, was fired on the grounds of her gender.

Under the leadership of Paige Patterson, the seminary's current president, who was hired after Klouda became a professor, the school is returning to a "'traditional, confessional and biblical position' that women should not instruct men in theology or biblical languages," according to Van McClain, chairman of the Southwestern trustees.[9]

These steps do not come without a price. Some consider such acts as an affront both to the traditions of the church and to biblical teaching. In a recent interview, bishop of Rochester, England, Michael Nazir-Ali, said, "Nobody wants a split [in the church], but if you think you have virtually two religions in a single church, something has got to give sometime."[10]

In a postdenominational world that divides more along lines of ideology and orthodoxy rather than church affiliation, one can hardly imagine a church that will do anything but grow further apart. Though few within the greater church wish this divide to happen, it appears to be inevitable. If we maintain traditional standards upon which the historical church was built, we risk greater alienation, a lingering sense of oppressiveness, and further cultural disconnection. If we press forward toward a vision of church within which gender, ethnicity, and sexual orientation are not criteria for ministry, we risk any number of divisions that could further weaken ailing religious institutions.

Where do we even begin to discern what God seeks from those who claim to be disciples of the Christian faith? Some believe religion's responsibility is to draw the boundaries of propriety within which the rest of society should operate. Others feel their spiritual calling is to step across some of these same lines, drawing cries of heresy from the ones making the rules.

Drawing Lines, Crossing Lines

This moral tension changes form over time, but it never goes away. Siddhartha Gautama shocked his stewards by leaving the safety of his father's palace to become the Buddha. Jesus challenged the authority of the Pharisees to the point that they played an integral part in his arrest, trial, and crucifixion. The price of taking such positions is seldom insignificant. However, for some, a church that does not face these kinds of social issues head-on does not earn the right to claim the gospel as its heritage.

The most divisive of these issues is homosexuality. In their book, *Caught in the Crossfire: Helping Christians Debate Homosexuality,* Sally Geis and Donald Messer suggest: "We need to perceive [scripture] not childishly but with a childlike faith."[11] Unfortunately, we Christians often take strong positions on this and other issues before we even have a proper vocabulary to employ to develop constructive dialogue. We generally consider homosexuality to be a single monolithic issue, and we debate whether or not it is a genetically predetermined and innate state of being or whether it is learned environmentally, adopted due to traumatic experiences or even by way of genetic mutation. When we achieve an arm's-length degree of objectivity, we quickly begin to see how such issues cannot be distilled down to an either/or debate we can so easily categorize. Geis and Messer offer a clear example of this in discussing several varieties of homosexual expression, which we consider briefly below:

- *Developmental homoerotic activity:* Takes place in children and adolescents of both sexes before adulthood;
- *Pseudo-homosexuality:* Indicated by same-sex relationships based upon dependence-independence and/or power-powerlessness rather than sexual desire;
- *Situational homosexuality:* Occur in captive same-sex populations, such as in prisons;
- *Enforced/exploitative homosexuality:* Happens in a relationship where one person exploits another individual;
- *Variational homosexuality:* Examples of this include prostitution;
- *Bisexuality:* Someone identifies themselves as gay or lesbian, but also continues to have heterosexual relations;
- *Ambisexuality:* Finding equal sexual pleasure from persons of either sex;
- *Ideological/political homosexuality:* Practiced by women who view sex with men as capitulation;
- *Preferential/exclusive homosexuality:* Identified with adults whose emotional and physical responses to adults of the same sex are preferred when there are no restrictions on availability of potential partners.[12]

In general, society equates the word *homosexuality* only with the last definition listed above. However, simply by considering these categories of homosexual expression, we begin to see how our subjective opinions, regardless of our position, may be based upon a less than complete understanding of the potential issues involved.

Several myths surround homosexuality, feeding divisive attitudes as well. For example, one myth is that most gay or lesbian people are pedophiles. However, the Kempe National Center for Prevention and Treatment of Child Abuse claims that only 2.5 percent of the offenders they see are identified as homosexual.[13] This percentage is significantly lower than national estimates of the gay and lesbian population in America, estimated to be between 10 and 15 percent of the overall population.[14] Other myths about gay and lesbian people enforce existing deep-seated emotional stances.

Though we have noted in other chapters that the largest contingency of American Evangelical Protestants are young adults, we also have pointed out that one cannot assume to know their social and political inclinations, simply based upon their church affiliation. In a January 2007, report titled, *How Young People View Their Lives, Futures and Politics: A Portrait of "Generation Next,"* the Pew Research

Center notes not only that today's young adults are increasingly liberal in their social and political views, but that the trend becomes only more pronounced the younger people are.

Whereas 47 percent of those surveyed over the age of twenty-five say they voted for John Kerry in the 2004 presidential election, and 52 percent voted for George Bush, 56 percent between the ages of eighteen and twenty-five voted for Kerry, and only 43 percent supported Bush. Regarding homosexuality, 50 percent of those surveyed aged twenty-six and older say it should be accepted, while 39 percent say it should be discouraged. Within the eighteen to twenty-five age group, 58% say homosexuality should be accepted, while less than one third feel it is something to discourage.[15]

When asked about the habits of today's young adults compared to young people twenty years ago, 75 percent of people surveyed between the ages of eighteen and twenty-five say today's young adults have more casual sex. Seventy percent say today's young people resort to violence more, 69 percent think their peers binge drink more, and nearly two thirds believe they use more illicit drugs now than did young people two decades ago.[16]

Some might hold these two sets of data next to one another and draw a direct correlation, suggesting that the liberalized culture of today's young adults leads directly to the erosion of moral values and subsequent behavior. Others perceive this generation as a group of young people who are compassionate and tolerant of differences, but who have great concerns for their future. In addition, the data suggest to some that young adults lack a sense of hope for their own peer group and that they lack a sense of belonging, strong leadership, and capable mentoring to help guide them toward the hope they would seek for themselves.

Eric's Story

I am male. I am white. I am a Christian. I am gay.

These are not all of the labels attached to me. I carry so many labels with me that I feel like one of those trunks you see in old movies that have stickers on them from all over the world. Personally, I haven't been around the world, but I have been "around."

I don't mind labels. Some people say we shouldn't use them. At this point in my life, I say *Why not?* Everything is replete with labels. Until we learn to communicate with only hearts and minds, we'll use labels to describe ourselves.

Some people would also say that the last two labels, Christian and gay, don't go together. They say those two stickers shouldn't be on the same trunk. I disagree.

I'm way past arguing the biblical side of homosexuality. Everyone uses the Bible to promote his or her own side of things, and those arguments are never won. Bible beating is an endeavor I leave to those who are happy doing it. Believe me, I've been beaten with a few Bibles. Those verses don't scare me anymore. What scares me are people who think what they read in a few obscure biblical passages gives them the right to judge and condemn me. What I find even scarier is that some people out there want to send me to hell.

For the past week, I have been in the place where I grew up. I left here over five years ago to attend seminary. Being here has brought back a lot of memories. I've relived good times, thought about bad times, and revisited some old dreams I'd forgotten about.

I've cried a lot since I've been here. It's been nearly two years since my last visit. Being with my parents fills me with emotion. I love them so much I physically hurt. Last night, when I kissed my mom goodnight, I left the room and cried. I have missed her embrace, the touch of her hands, and the sound of her voice. Seeing my father go about his daily tasks in the yard brings tears to my eyes.

I cry because I love them, and I cry because they do not know me. My parents taught me how to be a good Christian and how to be a good southerner. For them, these basically are the same thing. They taught me to work hard, be polite, and tell the truth, unless it might hurt someone's feelings. We did not argue. We didn't work things out around the dinner table. Silence is our mantra, and uncomfortable subjects are best left alone.

When I told my parents I was gay, they were shocked. I guess they thought all straight men spend a month's salary to attend Barbra Streisand's "final" concert. They asked me not to talk about it. I practically begged them to discuss it with me, but they refused. For years now, we have tiptoed around the subject. It's a little like ignoring a huge hunk of spinach in someone's teeth, though the consequences are more agonizing. The main reason, I think, is that they can't understand how my decision to enter the ministry can exist alongside my sexual orientation. They aren't the only ones.

One of my best friends was mortified when I decided to go to seminary. "How can you be a gay preacher?" she screamed at me. She was unable to get her mind around the concept.

I saw her over the weekend while I was back home. She told me that she had grown so much since that argument. As a matter of fact, she said that she would even be okay if her own son turned out to be gay. "I'd much rather him be gay than to marry a woman outside of his own race," she declared.

Faith journeys are difficult enough under the best of circumstances. When it seems no one thinks you are good enough to travel the road with them, it feels impossible.

When I was in seminary, I got a job at a church as the choir director. After being there a year, I decided I was tired of hiding a part of myself from the people I worked with and those I served in ministry. I came out of the closet at a board meeting, fully prepared to be asked to leave. Instead, I was loved and accepted. The board agreed to sponsor me for my application into the ordination process. I thought things had come full circle, but my journey of recognition for my call to ministry was far from complete.

As a child, I was not popular at school. I had few friends and was an outsider of sorts. At church, I finally felt important. At church, my gifts were celebrated. At church, I was somebody. It was a safe place. Jesus loved me, and so did Mrs. Brenda, Mrs. Linda, and Mr. Jack.

Those roles began to switch, however, as I became aware of my sexual orientation. I knew that gay people went to hell, and I didn't want to be one, but I couldn't help it. Anyone who claims homosexuality is a choice obviously doesn't understand how crazy you'd have to be to choose to be gay in a culture that rejects you outright. If another person out there has prayed and wished more than I to be "normal," I'd like to meet them. Church became a place where I looked over my shoulder. It became a chore. I knew the love there was conditional. If they really knew who I was, they wouldn't love me anymore.

In college and seminary, I met people who took my sexual orientation for granted. That sounds negative, but it isn't. Straight people have their sexuality taken for granted every day. School became a place where I could be free to be myself.

The circle had not come all the way around yet. When my new church's board approved my ordination candidacy, several families left the church. It's difficult to know that you are responsible for people leaving your congregation. However, the senior ministers and church leadership stood beside me.

I was not accepted into the ordination process by the larger church. It was a response I expected, but hearing the words hurt. It was like a slap across the face: sharp, painful, stinging. That feeling still lingers.

Some of the committee's leaders had encouraged me not to reveal my sexual orientation. The region where I live has a curious protocol that, although they will not revoke an ordained minister's standing for being openly gay, they will not ordain someone who admits to this during the ordination process. It's the good old "don't ask, don't tell" approach. But if I had it to do over again, I would do it the same way.

How can one enter the ministry of Jesus Christ under the pretense of a lie? I've played the silence game my entire life, but the game is painful. I have realized I am not ashamed to be a gay Christian, but other people are ashamed of me being one. As far as I'm concerned, that's their problem. I know I have gifts and graces for ministry. If I feel God's call to minister to people, I don't need a ceremony and a piece of paper to do it. I would rather be an unordained minister who is comfortable and honest with himself instead of an ordained one who has to pretend to be something he's not. Looking over my shoulder gives me neck cramps, anyway.

About once a week, however, I think about moving on to a new profession. How many times does an undergraduate get blackballed at the fraternity before he realizes he's not wanted there?

Then I think about Jesus. In my mind, he usually looks like he did when he was stuck to a felt board in Mrs. Brenda's Sunday school class. I remember that religious authorities did not accept him either. I remember that those closest to him did not understand him. Remembering makes me a better minister.

I don't have a "Jesus complex," but I do believe that if I had not been gay, I would not have entered the ministry. I would probably have married, had children, built a house on my parents' land, and lived there to this day. That's not a bad way to live, but being a gay Christian has taught me to be true to myself and to others, even if it hurts their feelings. It has taught me the true meaning of the gospel. It has taught me to love so much that it hurts, even when that love isn't always returned in full.

Staying at the Table

Clearly, homosexuality is one of the most divisive religious issues we currently face. The Episcopal Church is on the brink of a national split, based principally on this concern. Numerous congregations from every denomination have divided over differing positions on homosexuality, and gay rights have become a topic for heated national public debate. Some, such as Mary Lou Makepeace, executive director of the Gay and Lesbian Fund for Colorado, consider this discussion to be a catalytic moment for American culture. "Civil rights for gay men and lesbians is the civil rights issue of our time,"[17] she says. In this spirit, Makepeace and her organization have set out to do something about it.

Colorado Springs, home to the headquarters for Focus on the Family, Ted Haggard's New Life Church, and a number of other conservative groups, was the site for an ecumenical summit about homosexuality. In February 2007, more than one hundred religious leaders and thinkers from across the sociopolitical spectrum came together for three days to discuss homosexuality and the church in a respectful, thoughtful environment. The purpose of the event was to begin engaging in constructive dialogue about something that threatens to divide an already weakened Christian community.

Despite how one feels about sexuality with respect to scripture, dealing with this issue matter-of-factly is in our best interest as Christians. For some, it's a moral wedge issue. For others, it's a call to justice and equality. The idea that both sides will take the time to discourse about their beliefs and even their differences is critical to our sustainability as a cohesive body of faith.

Though Makepeace's organization helped coordinate the event, they avoided dictating the format and content of the summit. This hands-off approach, she says, allowed church leaders to feel free to bring their own perspectives and experiences to the event, rather than simply following the lead of a particular group with an inherent bias. "The ministry is on the front lines addressing this issue with families and individuals on a daily basis," says Makepeace, "but may be lacking the tools to comfortably have a discussion. By participating in this open dialogue, we hope people will find that they are better able to engage in conversations around some really tough issues related to relationships and the church."[18]

Ultimately, we choose whether or not agreeing to disagree, with an amicable willingness to coexist, is good enough. For real healing to take place, we must endeavor not only to remain in dialogue about sexuality as a conceptual abstraction, but we give it flesh and bone by recognizing the human lives that rest at the heart of these emotionally charged opinions. Though summits such as these are only one small step toward this type of awareness, such intentional time together offers hope. It suggests that some Christians are still willing to share a table together, even if they don't see eye to eye. Ultimately, we must decide if being right is more important than being available, and if justifying our personal convictions is more essential than welcoming all to our table to share in God's grace.

Do youth and young adults need someone in their lives who can impart values from a position of moral authority and conviction more than they need people with whom they can identify, share, and engage in discourse about the issues in their lives? The debate about the qualifications and criteria for leaders in ministry is far from over and may ultimately lead to the dissolution of many denominations and churches as we currently know them. We have two choices in facing this reality. We may stand firm with our own personal ideals, refusing to consider alternative points of view. We also can come around the table, welcoming those of all points of view, to discuss our differences with the goal of reconciliation and mutual enrichment. The future of the church depends on this choice.

Church of the Prodigal Child

Historically, families joined a local church, and for generations to come, their progeny followed in their steps, considering Sunday a sacred day. Children today, if not raised in the church, will have no context in which to access it from personal experience. In short, church is no longer a given. Without a paradigmatic shift in the church's approach to evangelism, generations to follow may never have church as a part of their heritage and their story.

The church, however, does have an opportunity to reach millions of young people who have some church background, but who have left or been marginalized for any number of reasons. We have the opportunity to celebrate their return, but to do so we must come to them with open arms and a ready table. The phrase "spiritual but not religious" is used to the point of cliché, yet it is a window we as church leaders must reach through, actively seeking to validate and cultivate the longing of those who have left to belong.

In this chapter, we learn the stories of a couple, with a young child, who no longer attend church. We listen to when and why they departed from organized religion and what they would want the church to look like if they ever decided to return. We will also see what they consider to be the role of spirituality in the lives of their children and what the church could do to help meet these families where they are. In a broader context, we will consider some of the history of so-called alternative spirituality in America, as well as some data we gathered from our online survey of more than 750 young adults.

Who Are They?

One of the challenges in developing this book concept was how best to reach young adults and engage them about their views in ways that were not proscriptive, too time-consuming or expensive. We decided on two methods for data gathering: an online survey and documentary-style storytelling and interviews on video.

Though both approaches yielded exciting and refreshing information, both also presented their own drawbacks. Though the video research was more expensive, the online survey had assets and liabilities as well. The greatest strengths of this approach were low cost and the ease of spreading the word about how to participate. For twenty dollars a month, we developed our survey on SurveyMonkey. com. From there, we sent links to the survey to our e-mail address books, posted it in online discussion forums, and spread it throughout many social networks on MySpace. Within a couple of weeks, hundreds of people had logged in to offer their opinions. Within two months, more than 700 people had participated. Had we attempted to replicate this project with a paper-based survey, it would have required thousands of dollars and at least a year of research time.

We were pleased with the age and geographic distribution of those who responded. A minimum of eight people responded at every age between eighteen and forty, with a higher concentration between eighteen and thirty years old, which we expected. Only five states had no representation in our survey: Alaska, Hawaii, Delaware, South Dakota, and Nevada. Just over 93 percent of respondents were residents of the United States, which was appropriate, given that the United States was the focus of our research.

The demographic bias also had some drawbacks. Nearly 89 percent of respondents identify themselves as Anglo, while only 5.6 percent identify themselves as of Latino descent, 3.8 percent African American, 3 percent Native American, and 1.7 percent Asian. Part of this likely is due to the disproportionate Anglo presence online, as well as the reality that we are both Anglos and the majority of our acquaintances are also Anglo. A report for the Leadership Conference on Civil Rights Education Fund titled "Are We Really a Nation Online? Ethnic and Racial Disparities in Access to Technology and Their Consequences" states that "blacks and Latinos are much less likely to have access to home computers than are white, non-Latinos (50.6 and 48.7 percent compared to 74.6 percent). They are also less likely to have Internet access at home

(40.5 and 38.1 percent compared to 67.3 percent)."[1] Churches should be aware of such ethnic, as well as other socioeconomic, biases that an online presence presents, if indeed their mission is to reach the community as a whole.

Also, though we had a broad geographic representation in our survey results, we noticed a bias toward Colorado and Texas, where we have the most personal connections. As we would send the survey link to our friends and family, they would send it on to those in their address book, many of whom live close to them. Despite the efficiency of this means of spreading the word, it hardly represents the entire country with respect to concentration of population.

Along these same lines, we received a disproportionately-large response from those identifying with our denomination, the Christian Church (Disciples of Christ). Though only approximately 500,000 Disciples live in America, more than 29 percent of those responding to our request were Disciples. Finally, we received unexpectedly high numbers of responses from agnostics and atheists. The story behind this is worth telling.

Christian is an active MySpace user and a member of several online discussion forums there. When creating the survey, we agreed it might be worthwhile to include both those who considered themselves "spiritual but not religious," as well as people who identified themselves as either atheist or agnostic. In that spirit, Christian joined an agnostic and atheist discussion group and posted an invitation to the group to take the survey. The response was both unexpectedly high and predictably bitter. Though many participated without complaint and even thanked us for the effort to reach beyond our comfort zones, a healthy group took significant issue with the content of the survey. Some were more respectful than others in their feedback, but the essential message was "these questions are so biased, we can't even complete the survey." Though nearly three fourths of all of the agnostic respondents completed the entire survey, just over 60 percent of atheists finished.

The complete survey results can be found on Christian's Web site (www.christianpiatt.com), but for the purposes of this chapter, we will consider the responses of the group who considered themselves "spiritual, but without any religious affiliation." Of the 765 initial participants, 94 (roughly one out of eight) selected this identification. More than three fourths of these completed the entire survey, which was within one percentage point of the overall average completion rate.

With regard to influences on their faith, the "spiritual but not religious" group, who we'll call the spiritual group for brevity, responded much like the overall averages with respect to people and their impact. However, the influence of both the Bible and church were significantly lower. Whereas 38 percent of all respondents said both the Bible and church strongly shaped their faith, only 6 percent of the spiritual group identified with these influences. Only 3 percent of the spiritual group attends church on a weekly basis, with most visiting church once or twice a year, or only for special events such as weddings and funerals. Less than 20 percent say their beliefs align with biblical teaching, less than 15 percent identify their beliefs with a certain church, and less than 10 percent feel any denomination echoes their views.

More than four in ten from the spiritual group had their initial church experience more than twenty years ago, with another 40 percent not claiming any church attendance history at all. Less than 10 percent began attending church fifteen years ago or less, which suggests most who have attended church did so as young children first. This idea is supported by the claim made by nearly 86 percent of the spiritual group that family took them or invited them to their first church encounter. The number of respondents from this group who had a positive experience their first time at church was only slightly lower than the average (74 percent versus 79 percent), but they took longer to decide whether or not they would return to church. Though just more than 20 percent of the overall respondents took a year or more to decide whether or not they would continue to attend church, the rate for the spiritual group was nearly double this (38 percent).

Though the spiritual group spends only slightly less time in weekly prayer or meditation than the average, they spend significantly less time with scripture. However, one out of three reports spending at least half an hour each week reading the Bible. Not entirely surprising is that they have a relatively negative outlook on church. Less than 30 percent believe churches are necessary or healthy, and less than one in ten feels churches are responsible with money or important to their lives. Only 15 percent think the programs churches offer are relevant to them, yet an unexpected 49 percent say churches are still places of comfort.

The spiritual group is not dissimilar from the overall group in many respects about what they think the focus of church should be.

Though worship and evangelism did not rank as highly important, issues such as social activism (85 percent), fellowship/community (77 percent), prayer, and moral issues (both 58 percent) were seen as "essential" or "very important." They tend to see church principally as judgmental (92 percent), intimidating (61 percent), and frightening (52 percent), though a significant number also view church in general as available (73 percent), strong (65 percent), energetic (47 percent), and engaged (45 percent).

Almost three fourths believe it's acceptable to question and doubt in church, but only one in five believes their opinions can be heard there. Ninety-five percent strongly feel everyone should be welcome in church, no matter what, yet few seem to think this reflects the climate of modern church. More than 80 percent say churches overstep their political limits.

Some from the spiritual group have positive religious associations with direct personal church encounters (57 percent), other church-going family members (50 percent), or friends (38 percent). Negative feelings generally come from the same places, but to a much stronger degree. Eighty-seven percent have had negative personal experiences, and 90 percent associate negative feelings with other religious people. Seventy percent also form negative views of religion from what they find in the media.

Around 80 percent have positive associations with the terms *God* and *prayer*, and 64 percent have a positive view of Jesus. However, less than one in five from this group sees churches as positive institutions, and denominations don't fare even half that well. The spiritual group is also less likely to volunteer than the average, and they give substantially less to charity. Though 95 percent have a desire to grow spiritually, church is not seen as the best place for this to take place. Nearly 80 percent of those who have had a negative experience with church say that encounter now affects their church attendance, whereas only half of the overall group experiencing something negative at church reports that it affects their involvement.

They are, however, just as likely to attend church as the average respondent if the church offers what they see as relevant programs or services, and they are equally willing to share their views on spirituality. They generally perceive God as ever-present (78 percent), loving (68 percent), omniscient (64 percent), and merciful (52 percent).

These statistics suggest that those churches that can outwardly demonstrate an openness to nonthreatening spiritual dialogue and that also reflect a God image of a present, loving, and merciful God have an opportunity to connect with this spiritually hungry group. This group would find most appealing a commitment to social justice issues, a strong sense of community, and an emphasis on prayer. At the same time, the church should avoid an atmosphere of judgment and overt involvement in political issues.

Much of the other results in the survey for the spiritual group reflect our overall findings. We learn from all this that those who feel a distinct spiritual connection but who do not feel involved with church are not entirely dissimilar from the young people already attending. Their values and perceptions of church are not far apart, though more of them have allowed a hurtful experience to come between them and a community of faith. Community outreach efforts and taking positions on matters of justice such as poverty and the environment are more important to them than having the church impart moral values.

Perhaps most important is that they are open to God's presence in their lives, and they are willing to engage in meaningful dialogue, prayer, and study about faith. Though traditional church worship settings may not immediately provide the greatest opportunity for bridging these gaps and reconciling some of the damage that may have been done, small group contacts outside of the church and one-on-one relationships provide the greatest opportunity for rebuilding the trust upon which a healthy corporate faith experience can be built.

Brenda and Sam's Story

Brenda and Sam live in Fort Worth, Texas. They are both in their mid-thirties, and they have one son, Jared. They are both active in sports, and they have a wide circle of friends. Sam, a computer programmer, started a computer consultancy with a friend of his in 2006, and Brenda, a nurse anesthetist, also has her own business. Both are college educated and have some history with the Christian church. Neither currently attends any church, and we asked them to share some about their experiences with and thoughts about church and faith.

Brenda: "I grew up in a small town, didn't go to church, and my parents didn't go to church. Spirituality was not really an issue at our house. We didn't pray before meals. I do remember being excited about breaking out the manger scene at Christmas time, but we didn't even attend church at Christmas. We just listened to records and that kind of stuff. So, religion didn't really play a part.

"We did have some friends that were very—I don't know if I want to say, 'religious.' I grew up in big Mormon community. My best friend was Mormon. I did go to a few [church activities], like Vacation Bible School, where you make the birdhouse out of popsicle sticks, and learned songs like 'Deep and wide, deep and wide, there's a fountain flowing deep and wide.' That was my religious history. And then, I guess I was looking for something. I don't know; I guess everybody's looking for something when they're teenagers.

"Church was a huge part of one of my best friends' life because she was a minister's daughter. We always ended up at the church for one thing or another. Her church was what I would look for in a church now if I ever go to church. It was a smaller place—a very welcoming place. People noticed if you were there or not there.

"Her dad, the minister, always had great sermons. For me, they were great because they were always so relatable. He would take a story from everyday life, whether it was an experience in his life, or something that he'd read about. I guess that they were mostly personal experiences. And then, he would select some scripture, tell the story, and relate the two. It was always some sort of take-home message, like 'care about people,' or 'be kind to one another.' There was no fire and brimstone involved.

"I remember, one time the minister was out of town, and we had a visiting preacher. He made us get down on our knees, which was odd. He was saying, 'Give up your life to God! You have no control, because it's all in God's plan.' That really turned me off. I'll be honest with you. To this day, I don't believe that. I think it's kind of a cop out, to say, 'Well, just leave it up to God.'

"My junior or senior year of high school I started attending that church every week. It brought me a lot. It was a good service every week; sort of made you take time out every week to think about the greater good and God. It's so easy to get caught up in day-to-day stuff. The moment of silence that they always give you…allows you to think about the people that you care about and the people that you know that are going through tough times and could use a little support. Anyway, I haven't gone to church since then."

Sam: "I was born Roman Catholic. Growing up, I went to catechism, got christened, you know, all that stuff. My mom was Catholic, and I think my dad was Presbyterian, but I wouldn't know because we never went to a Presbyterian church. My dad didn't really go to church very often with us...so my mom would take us.

"When I was in second grade, my parents sent us to Southwest Christian, which was a Church of Christ school. We had chapel and Bible study class every day. The Church of Christ does not believe in instruments in church. For some reason, they decided that it was inappropriate in church. You could only sing a capella, which was actually kind of cool for me because I didn't play instruments and I could sing all right.

"One of the things that I always remembered from going to school there was that they always said that it was a nondenominational school, even though they sponsored it. All the teachers were members of that church and almost everybody that went there was too. They taught their beliefs. That was a really big factor in turning me off from organized religion. They were very 'We're right, you're wrong, and if you believe the way we do, then you're going to go to heaven. If you don't, then we're not going to judge you, because it's wrong to judge, but you're just going to hell. It is your choice if you want to do that...but, the Bible says that you're going to hell.' I always thought that was really odd. So I ended up kind of being pretty antiestablishment."

Around Sam's eight or ninth grade year, his parents decided they should find a church where the entire family could worship together. They visited an independent Bible church one particular Sunday, though his family didn't end up attending this church. Years later, he recalls driving by this same church and seeing an antiabortion rally in front, with young children holding signs bearing graphically violent images and dolls of dead babies hanging from ropes. He claims it made him angrier than he's ever been. The experience contributed to his growing skepticism about the authenticity of the church as a whole and its commitment to a message of compassion and peace.

Sam: "We ended up in the Methodist church. It was an awesome church experience. It was great. The pastor there was really funny. He was down to earth. He told a lot of personal stories and integrated them into the religion. We went to youth group. My first ski trip was with the youth group in a bus that we drove to Crested Butte. I changed schools in ninth grade, and my social scene changed.

Everybody picked on me. But at church, people didn't pick on me. I had my first girlfriend there. It was fun. To make a long story short, church was my social scene. I had friends and it helped me.

"Like most college kids, waking up on Sunday was pretty tough for me. Church just drifted away. When the pastor left, it just wasn't the same. He went off the deep end, lost it, got a divorce, and sold used cars. It's kind of interesting, that there's the guy that you really look up to, and then his life falls apart. I guess that has something to do with my perception of church.

"I took a world religion class in college. It was eye opening. I started asking myself 'Why would Western religion be the right one? Why are we better than the other ones?' I think my current status is that I'm agnostic. I do believe in a higher power, but I don't really know what that is. Obviously, nobody does. I don't necessarily believe in the whole 'Jesus is the Son of God' story. I don't believe in any one religion, but I think there's something there. Another part of me says this is all made up.

"You see the things in nature, and it doesn't make sense that that all happened for no reason. I try not to condemn or accept any one denomination or type of religion. I think that if you're happy in your religion that's great, and I just try to learn a little bit from everybody. My relationship with God is personal. I actually sometimes pray, I think, kind of. A lot of times it's when I'm in a really bad situation. Like, 'Oh, God, if you just help me here, then…' Everybody does that sometimes, and I fall into that category too."

Brenda: "When I first came to college, I actually considered going to church. I actually got up and tried to go. I was very intimidated when I saw all of the churchgoers in the dorm cafeteria on Sunday morning. That sealed the deal. People were decked out to go to church! It was culture shock coming from a small town. I felt so out of place. And that was it for me, as far as religion goes.

"Living in the Bible Belt, it seems like the most intolerant people are the most religious people. The people you hear making racial comments appear to be the most religious. That's just depressing. I mean, what's the point? I think religion is important for a lot of people, for a lot of cultures. It provides social mores. It provides some structure for civilization. It's hard for us to imagine what it would be like to not understand things like how the body works or why people die. To have a greater power that can explain all of that for you is probably necessary for some people just to get through life. I think we're at a place in civilization — on a grander scale, if you look way back in the day when you didn't understand how things worked, you had no clue, and your life completely sucked because you got up in the morning and you busted your butt all day long trying to live.

"Religion's got to be some kind of evolutionary coping mechanism that helps you find some purpose for being here. When you think about people who are clinically depressed, it's because their life has no purpose. Their life is meaningless. If you look at religion, what's it do for people? 'You got to live for tomorrow, because you got to get into heaven and that's where you're going to spend the rest of eternity, for God's sake. So, you'd better be good now.' I think that's what's important for a lot of people. It's hard for me to imagine why religion hasn't evolved a little more.

"It's hard for me to understand how people can take a book that was written [so long ago] and not be able to look at things objectively. It was written by men, you know. And it's been translated how many times? And you're saying that people didn't impress their own opinions and feelings on it, but yet you're going to take that literally, even now? It just seems ignorant, frankly. I guess religion is great for a lot of people. Faith is great for a lot of people. It's probably great for most people, but not all people.

"We have a son now, who's eighteen months old. I think I want him to experience some kind of church setting. You know, the way Sam describes his experience with church and the church family that I experienced, for however short of time, at the Disciples church. It's a great place for people.

"Sam's mom is a great example of how church can help people. She was devastated when his father left her, and the people gathered around her and supported her. They still support her. Her church family is huge for her. She goes to church every Sunday. She's very involved. It's a great thing. She's one of those people whose faith is very personal. She goes to Bible study, but you never hear her talk about it. She never tries to impress it on you. She just lives it. To me, she's a good example of a religious success story."

Sam: "There are tons of religious success stories."

Brenda: "We have a friend who is the classic, hypocritical, die-hard Christian. She cannot forgive her ex-boyfriend, but she'd be glad to quote you a little scripture. Then we have friends who are straight up atheists, who don't believe in anything, except for 'Here we are. Let's make the most of it.'

"I don't know if I'm an atheist. I think I'm more of an agnostic. I don't know. I don't believe in an afterlife. I think people die and that's it. But, we have to believe in an afterlife because it's too difficult to imagine going through what we go through and then just having it end. But I don't think that means necessarily that I don't believe in a Higher Power. I would say that I am a little bit remiss, and I guess we all are, because sometimes all you can do is get up in the morning and get it all done before you go to bed. I would like to educate myself, especially because of our son, read some more, try to figure out what I think, and maybe get a little bit better understanding about things. I envy people who have time to reflect and pray. I think that's really cool. I don't know that it would be anything that I would necessarily do. I don't feel like I'm lacking anything, but it would be nice to be on the same page as a couple."

Sam: "I think religion has a less predominant role for young adults in general than when I was younger. Then, as a parent you start thinking, 'OK, I'm going to raise this child, and I want to impart values and morals in his life.' The most common way values and morals are imparted into peoples' lives is by going to church. So if you don't go to church, you have to impart those morals yourself. I've always been of the opinion that morals are just morals. They're not religiously based. Religion teaches morals, just like normal people teach morals. Morality is a way of keeping people civilized. So, if you don't have morality or laws, you have chaos and anarchy.

"My mom will play religious songs for our son. I like religious songs. At some point, he's going to question what these things mean. And I'm going to have to come up with some kind of answers for what I believe. I don't want to impart my beliefs on him, but I don't want to blindly lead him somewhere. Everything you learn as a kid is a foundation for everything else in your life. I don't want to put him in a situation where he's got bad information, or in a situation where he has no information. I think we probably will decide that we need to go to a church or some kind of an organization that he can be a part of, that can help him with some of those questions and develop his own philosophy. I think it would be good for us in general."

Brenda: "I definitely think church of some sort is a positive thing. A huge thing that I want to do and don't do enough of is volunteer work and charity work. We are so fortunate in our lives, we are just–I sound like a Southerner–blessed. We have a lot. That's something that we need to give back for one reason or another. When you think about charity, you always associate it with church-based things. Churches do help people. That's what they're there for–for lost souls. So, not only to try to give our son some kind of a foundation, it wouldn't hurt us to go and evaluate what our personal morals are once a week for an hour.

"A Unitarian church will probably be an interesting place for us to start. I'm surrounded by hard-core, right-wing Christians all day long in my work, and because it's my work, I can't talk about it. Also, I don't feel like I'm educated enough to discuss with them. The point is I can see us someday choosing to go to church. I don't really feel like I am lacking in morals. I don't think it made me a better or worse person. It was just a nonfactor for me."

Sam: "Yeah, we'll check out the Unitarian church sometime. I think we are more liberal than conservative, so that might work out."

Jake on the Church

We asked Jake, who shared his story in the chapter titled "Addiction," about his views regarding what the church does well and what work it has yet to do in order to successfully serve the young adult community. As someone who came to church later in life, he has been on both sides of the spiritual paradigm. Following are some of his thoughts regarding the current church and its relationship to those beyond the walls:

"What we really need is more Bible study. When I read 'Joined in Discipleship,' a history of the Disciples of Christ, one of the things I noticed was that in the beginning of the restoration movement, there was a real strong emphasis on studying the word of God, personal responsibility, and a personal right to read and interpret the word for themselves.

"It seems that over the course of time, we didn't want to offend people because they had different beliefs, or maybe held to different doctrines. We restrained from pushing anything on anybody or have anything pushed on us, so we gave everybody the right to read scripture for themselves and understand it. I think it's progressed to the point now where we don't want to offend anybody at all, and we don't have any opinions any more.

"You look back at the Protestant Reformation, and the driving force behind that was to get the Bible back into the hands of the people so they could read and understand it for themselves. Acts 2 talks about how the early Christians dedicated themselves daily to breaking bread, prayer, and the apostles' teaching. What I see is that people have stopped reading the Word of God. It bothers me that people don't even seem to understand the basics of the gospel message.

"You do not need a seminary education to have a relationship with God. But I don't understand how it would be possible if you don't read the Bible. If you want to reach young adults, do it the way that it's always worked throughout history. We don't need to come up with something new. We don't need to give it a fancy name, or have church in a theater or a gymnasium. We just need to remember what's important. We need to teach people how to read scripture and understand it for themselves.

"Mentoring and discipleship groups are a good idea. A big thing that made a difference in my life was a Christian man coming alongside me. He lived a life of Christ. I understood by being around him the importance of prayer, the importance of reading the scriptures, and what it meant to worship.

"I like the idea of the Emerging Church...but I hate the idea of taking something that someone else has done, packaging it up, and trying to make it work where we're at. I'd much rather listen to God, listen to the leading of the Spirit, and be faithful to what God is calling our church to do.

"You see these guys like Rick Warren [who wrote] *The Purpose Driven Life*, Willow Creek, and all these 'seeker friendly' churches. I think what they're doing is great. What I don't like is when their books become best-sellers, and everybody in town tries to emulate what they're doing. I don't think it's a faithful call to ministry to try to reproduce what another leader has done...I think we need to find our own vision."

Regarding evangelism, "It's not something that's really talked about. We talk about finding more church members and about seeing people come to Christ. However, one thing that has been really weird for me in the Disciples of Christ denomination is seeing how everybody's related and going to big functions and seeing how everybody knows each other. It almost seems that you have to be born into the Disciples. It doesn't seem to be a need for people to share their faith.

"If you read the New Testament, there's a big emphasis on people sharing their faith. That's how the church has grown and survived. It's not about going out and doing a membership drive or knocking on people's doors, riding bicycles around. The church that's growing needs to be a church that's living out their faith, and part of that 'living out' is evangelism.

"When there are four or five churches in an area and they are looking at closing down, …we need to look at what we're not doing that we used to do. We need to look at what we're not doing that these Asian, Haitian, and Hispanic churches are doing. I'm sure that we'll find people willing to share their faith with their neighbors and their friends.

"We need to give the Word of God back to the People of God. It can't be the responsibility of just the pastor of a congregation to do that. Home fellowship leaders train others to lead a home fellowship. They model that; it works."

Spiritual but Not Religious

A seemingly paradoxical concept helps define a dynamic of today's youth and young adults: suffocating freedom. This phrase, or variations thereof, occurred in two separate books about young adults that we came across in our research. In the book *A Generation Alone: Xers Making a Place in the World,* William Mahedy and Janet Bernardi say that "when an entire generation of people feel (sic) that no decision they make will affect anyone else, the sense of freedom can be suffocating. That is aloneness."[2] In *Quarterlife Crisis: The Unique Challenges of Life in Your Twenties,* Alexandra Robbins and Abby Wilner share the stories of many twentysomething adults who are experiencing crises of identity generally associated with midlife. Andrea from Portland, Oregon, found within religion an opportunity to "escape from modern freedom: from the mandatory opportunity to discover what I really think about things, from the requirement to listen to my inner voice, from the rule that I learn to live my life on my own."[3]

Though Andrea was raised in the church by her parents, only in her twenties did she become "more serious and purposeful about her faith… I discovered that the narrative of God's love for God's people reveals a very different kind of freedom: the freedom to never again have to worry if I really am somebody."[4] In the same book, Sandra, who was a recent college graduate, describes the fear she has about the lack of limits in her life:

That's what's best about the twenties—we're so free. No mortgages, no kids, no job that we've been at for fifteen years.

The problem, though, as I've tried to explain a million times to my mom, is that freedom is a really big burden. When all the options are available, it's really easy to sit on your butt and choose nothing.[5]

Combine a lack of definition and boundary with a fundamental mistrust in the systems intended to support us, and the result is a toxic crisis of identity. More than half of the children from so-called "Generation X" have two parents who worked, and half of our parents' marriages ended in divorce. One third of them were either physically or sexually abused.[6] We've witnessed the dissolution of public trust in systems of government, religion, and capitalism. The message we hear from church is to rely on God rather than ourselves, to trust the church even if it has failed us in the past, and to put others first. However, these sentiments generally are antithetical to our worldview, and to the values imparted to us by our families of origin.

Despite the cynicism and self-protective defensiveness, this generation has a tremendous desire to ensure that our actions, decisions, and very lives mean something.[7] Andrea mentions above that she found this assurance in the church, but many young adults are unsure if this is the only, or even the best, avenue for discovering this sense of meaning, significance, and belonging we desperately seek.

There is a gross misperception that ours is a nation founded strictly on Christian principles and that in recent generations we have become increasingly secularized and further alienated from a sense of spirituality. Reality tells a much different story. In the 1600s, only one third of the American population attended church, and by the Revolutionary War, the number had dropped to 15 percent.[8] In his book, *Spiritual but Not Religious,* Robert Fuller notes that throughout American history we have been a people with "persistent interest in religious ideas that fall well outside the parameters of Bible-centered theology."[9] This not only applies to those outside the church; many within the Christian faith have traditionally held personal beliefs considered to be mystical, paranormal, or otherwise alternative in nature. This trend is consistently present today according to a recent Baylor religion study with more than 1,700 respondents.

Founding fathers such as John Adams, Benjamin Franklin, and Thomas Jefferson, all avowed Deists, not Christians, rejected the notion that the Bible contained revealed truth. This, they argued, was "unreasonable religion."[10] Jefferson went a step further, criticizing the "irrational nature of institutional religion."[11]

The Enlightenment era provided fertile soil for many alternative religious and philosophical practices, including Deism. Though not confined to a particular institutional set of doctrines or dogma, many of the principal tenets of Deism in particular had much in common with fundamental teachings of the Christian church: belief in a divinely created universe; belief in the immortality of the human soul; and an emphasis on moral living and ethical standards, such as charity.[12]

Five common themes characterize other American spiritual movements:

1. *Personal autonomy:* They value the individual's right to establish one's own criteria for belief. Religious doctrines are not simply accepted on faith, but rather are tested through real-world experience.
2. *Sensibility over creeds:* Religious truth is accepted only to the degree that it helps people connect with the divinity in all living creatures.
3. *Impatience with organized religion:* Churches are generally seen as stagnant and out of touch with the rest of the world. Those who are impatient also include a significant contingency that has been hurt, disappointed, or otherwise disenfranchised by religion.
4. *Present applicability:* They generally believe the greatest limitation of spiritual growth is not sin, but rather one's own limited awareness of one's potential as a spiritual being. Instead of focusing on the afterlife, alternative spiritual practices traditionally have focused on the fullness of present life.
5. *Fascination with the metaphysical:* Interest in the supernatural aspects of human experience and what lies beyond the physical universe.[13]

Though these trends have been identified throughout American alternative spiritual cultures for centuries, these same sentiments are common among those whom we surveyed and among those who consider themselves "spiritual but not religious."

Many points of intersection occur between Christians and those identifying with alternative spiritual paths. We all can generally agree on the idea of a divinely created universe and on the concept of the immortality of the soul. All agree that certain moral and ethical standards are necessary for a healthy, nurturing society, though we may not immediately agree about the details of what constitutes moral or ethical behavior.

Interestingly, many of the tenets of alternative spirituality listed above are those noted in the "Habit, Tradition, Ritual" chapter as characteristic of religious systems that are "mature" versus "immature," as well as those that contribute best to healthy personal development. Gordon Allport indicates the healthiest spiritual environment is differentiated, dynamic, and heuristic; offers consistent morality; and is both integral and comprehensive. Though we may have particular semantic differences as we engage in dialogue, the first goal is to create a climate conducive to healthy, mutually-respectful dialogue. Nothing is inherently antithetical in any of these alternative spiritual concepts that has to stand between us and those outside our doors, that is, unless we are intent only on being right and justifying our own point of view, rather than remaining open to the possibility that we as Christians might still have something to learn about spirituality too.

Finally, we must bear in mind the ultimate purpose of our efforts. Is success or failure only measured by church attendance; or if we can help bring healing, comfort, or greater understanding to someone's life, are our energies well spent? Are we manifesting the gospel message without expectation, or are we motivated, as many suspect, by the desire to grow our numbers, to feel more secure in the validation of the rest of the world seeing God as we do, or by shoring up our fiscal bottom line?

If Jesus is the model for our ministry and evangelism, we can quickly realize that getting people through the doors of church is not the point. The central thrusts of Jesus' ministry were to bring healing to a hurting world, to sit and share time and stories with those otherwise rejected by society, and then to charge those who found hope and nourishment in his teaching to carry it with them to the corners of the earth. In many ways, he was his culture's poster boy for "spiritual but not religious." People believed he was who he claimed to be not because he held a respectable position within the church or because he demonstrated authority through acts of overwhelming power. His life and how he connected with the world set him apart, and he didn't stand behind a pulpit to do it.

Conclusion

Wrapping up is something we as a culture don't do particularly well. We love a happy ending, but we often stretch to find one. From national elections to jury trials, we long for closure, but we get caught up in the drama and end up overwhelmed by the process. What we need is a sign of hope. Take the Olympics, for example. This is an event we open with a bang and conclude well. It includes ceremony and celebration, symbol and tradition. When the flame is finally extinguished, we always have a symbol of what is to come, a spark that will be tended. We look forward to the next time people will be gathered from around the world, and once again the fire will be lit.

We offer you this ember, a spark to take back to your congregations and communities to ignite their passions and inspire their hearts. Most important is the realization that you have a story worth telling. Regardless of your race, age, orientation, gender, or education, you have the capacity to help someone else by sharing your story.

Along with other young adults, we long for your wisdom and guidance. We seek to learn from your struggles, successes, and failures. We may not tell you outright, but we love you and appreciate you. We stand on your shoulders. The trouble is that sometimes we don't know how to ask for your help because we don't know what we need. We don't know if we can trust you, and we don't know if you really want to know us.

Churches offer us many ways to explore our faith, but we need companions for the journey. We want to hear about how you have dealt with the challenges of growing up, of discerning your call, your doubts, fears, and disappointments. Have you ever been mad at God? Have you ever denied God's existence? These are the ways that you show us you are a real person. We find comfort in knowing we are not alone. We like to hear that someone else has had these questions and has survived. We want to meet people who have lived to tell about it.

We need help getting over the notion that all you want to do is tell us what we are doing wrong. We need help finding our way to your door, so you'll probably need to come to us first. We still look to you as an example. You are our spiritual ancestors. We do care about you, even if we don't show it. If we seem angry, it's because many of us are. Show us that you can handle our anger. Give us opportunities to express it. Our appearance may frighten you. We may be tattooed and pierced, but under all that metal and ink is the same blood that pumps through your veins.

You may think you've lost us, but you have not. When you see us off in the distance, lingering along the fringes, drop what you're doing and run to us. Kill the fatted calf and throw us a party. Celebrate our stories too. We may have been gone for a long time, and we may have squandered most of our inheritance, but you have not forgotten who we are or to whom we belong. Remind us. Listen to us. Kindle the light you see in our eyes, and we will eventually see it too. Believe in us.

We don't need truth wrapped up in a nice little bow. We'd much rather have it generously shared within a sincere relationship, not from on high but from the heart. We know a phony when we see one. We also know when you are being real. We respond better to the latter. We crave authenticity. We want to know where our story fits in the greater scheme of things. We want to know that grace holds the world together, but we're just trying to get ourselves together. If you can accept this, you can help us. If you try to fix us, we will resent you. If you share with us about how you found hope, we will appreciate you.

We don't need fanfare as much as we need sacrament. We like some of your old prayers, and we even like some of your old songs. You don't need to forfeit who you are to let us be who we are. We don't really need a happy ending. Rather than happiness, God offers hope. Life is messy. We know that as well as you. Be the hope we seek.

You know how to make space for the sacred. We have become so concerned with remaining set apart that we have forgotten how to stay connected. We compete for space, while you seem to take it for granted. The fortress of faith from which you take comfort has become a barrier for us. You are on the inside, so you feel safe, but from the outside the church looks more like a barricade. Beat a path from your door to ours and, with a little light along the way, we'll find you. Let your light shine. We are curious. Sooner or later, if you tend the fire, we'll come and join you to share our story. Over time and with a little faith and effort, those stories will intertwine to be come part of the ongoing faith narrative of our predecessors and those who will come after us.

Help us reenvision what it means to experience the sacred. Let your faith out of the church box. Make time and room for the spontaneous sacred, wherever we find one another. Don't be afraid of the words we use to describe our faith. Hear what we mean, not just what we say. Instead of being critical because we don't know where we stand on every question, celebrate our willingness to sit at the same table. By honoring the divine spark you see in us, we learn to recognize it in ourselves. By asking us about our stories, we come to believe they are worth telling. By sharing stories of your own, we learn that we are not as alone as we think.

Notes

Introduction

[1]"The MySpace Generation," *BusinessWeek,* December 12, 2005.

[2]Michael Lewis, *Next: The Future Just Happened* (New York: W. W. Norton & Company, 2002).

[3]1 Corinthians 13:12

[4]Information obtained from http://www.barna.org/FlexPage.aspx?Page=BarnaUpdat e&BarnaUpdateID=101.

[5]Ibid.

[6]Ibid.

I Love to Tell the Story

[1]"Blog" is short for "Web log," an online diary which millions of people use to document personal thoughts and details about their lives, allowing friends or even the public at large to read their entries.

[2]Baylor Institute for Studies of Religion, *American Piety in the 21st Century: New Insights to the Depth and Complexity of Religion in the U.S.* (September, 2006), 4.

[3]Ibid., 4.

[4]Quotations obtained from http://dir.salon.com/story/mwt/col/lamott/2003/07/04/church/index.html.

[5]From the opening words of AA meetings.

[6]The Baylor study defines Evangelical Protestant churches as Anabaptist, Assemblies of God, Bible Church, Brethren, Christian Church, Christian and Missionary Alliance, Christian Reformed, Church of Christ, Church of God, Church of the Nazarene, Free Methodist, Lutheran Church-Missouri Synod, Mennonite, Pentecostal, Presbyterian Church in America, Seventh-Day Adventist, and Southern Baptist.

[7]David Hogue, *Remembering the Future, Imagining the Past: Story, Ritual, and the Human Brain* (Cleveland: The Pilgrim Press 2003), 90.

[8]Psalm 42:1b–2

[9]John 19:28

[10]Ernest Kurtz and Katherine Ketcham, *The Spirituality of Imperfection: Storytelling and the Search for Meaning* (New York: Bantam, 1993), 7.

[11]Ibid., 5–18.

[12]Hogue, *Remembering the Future, Imagining the Past,* 90.

[13]Ibid., 91.

[14]The Stations of the Cross tell the story of Jesus' crucifixion from Pontius Pilate's proclamation that Christ would be crucified to Jesus' death.

[15]Hogue, *Remembering the Future, Imagining the Past,* 76.

[16]Ibid.

The God Image

[1]Judy Woodruff, "Young People Express Views on Religion, Politics," *The News Hour with Jim Lehrer* (Jan. 3, 2007).

[2]Ibid.

[3]Baylor Institute for Studies of Religion, *American Piety in the 21st Century: New Insights to the Depth and Complexity of Religion in the U.S.* (September 2006), 7.

[4]Karen Armstrong, *A History of God: The 4,000-Year Quest of Judaism, Christianity, and Islam* (New York: Ballantine Books, 1993), 19.

[5]Ibid., 19.

[6]Franklin J. Woo, "God in Chinatown: Religion and Survival in New York's Evolving Immigrant Community," *China Review International* 10, no. 2 (2003).

[7]The terms *Evangelical* and *Mainline* are being used as defined in the Baylor study noted earlier.

[8]Kenneth J. Guest, *God in Chinatown: Religion and Survival in New York's Evolving Immigrant Community* (New York and London: New York University Press, 2003), 171–72.

[9]Baylor Institute for Studies of Religion, *American Piety in the 21st Century,* 11.

[10]Woo, "God in Chinatown."

[11]Will Lester, "Generation Next More Democratic," Associated Press, January 2007. Information available at http://www.chieftain.com/national/1168423897.

[12]Woodruff, "Young People Express Views."

[13]Baylor study, 15.

[14]Woodruff, "Young People Express Views."

[15]Ibid.

[16]Baylor study, 26–34.

[17]The full Baylor study can be downloaded for free at http://www.baylor.edu/isreligion/index.php?id=40634.

[18]Baylor study, 26.

[19]Ibid.

[20]Ibid., 27.

[21]Julie Carlson, "Losing My Religion? No, Says Baylor Religion Survey," press release, Baylor Institute for Studies of Religion, September 11, 2006.

[22]Baylor study, 28–29.

[23]Ibid., 30.

[24]Ibid., 29.

[25]Ibid., 30.

[26]Ibid.

[27]Ibid.

[28]Ibid., 32.

[29]G. Jeffrey MacDonald, "U.S. Churches Play up Fun to Attract Participants," *The Christian Science Monitor,* wire service, January 3, 2006.

[30]Ibid.

The Coffeehouse Myth

[1]Information obtained from http://en.wikipedia.org/wiki/Coffeehouse.

[2]Ibid.

[3]Ibid.

[4]Ibid.

[5]Information obtained from http://www.msnbc.com/id/15143850/..

[6]Information obtained from http://www.tableofgrace.org/vision.html.

[7]Tammy Alhadef, "Jesus and Java," *The Pueblo Chieftain,* August 26, 2006.

[8]Ibid., 30

Habit, Tradition, and Ritual

[1]Information obtained from http://www.sfgate.com/cgi-bin/article.cgi?f=/c/a/ 2006/01/15/RVG40GI9M71.DTL.

[2]Betty Lin-Fisher, "Debt Crushing Young Adults," *Akron Beacon Journal* (http://www.demos.org/pubs/debtakron.pdf).

[3]David Morris, "Lived Time and Absolute Knowing: Habit and Addiction from Infinite Jest to the Phenomenology of Spirit," *CLIO* 30, no. 4 (2001).

[4]Ibid.

[5]Ibid.

[6]Ibid.

[7]Terry Eagleton, "Rediscover a Common Cause or Die: We Used to Find Unity in a Shared Heritage. Yet We Are Set on Defining Our Difference," *New Statesman,* July 26, 2004.

[8]Martin Luther King Jr. speech, Western Michigan University, 1963.

[9]Eagleton, "Rediscover a Common Cause or Die."

[10]David Hogue, *Remembering the Future, Imagining the Past: Story, Ritual, and the Human Brain* (Cleveland: The Pilgrim Press, 2003), 116.

[11]Ibid., 117.

[12]Catherine Bell, *Ritual Theory, Ritual Practice* (New York: Oxford University Press, 1992), 3.

[13]Ibid., 47.

[14]Ibid.

[15]Ibid., 92.

[16]Ibid., 94.

[17]Information obtained from http://www.brenthouse.org/faith.html.

[18]Ibid.

[19]Lara M. Brown, "Game Master," *The New Yorker,* November 6, 2006, 94.

[20]Ibid., 94.

[21]Information obtained from http://www.brenthouse.org/faith.html.

[22]Hogue, *Remembering the Future, Imagining the Past,* 121.

[23]Ibid., 122–23.

[24]Ibid., 144.

[25]Ibid., 146.

[26]Ibid., 147.

[27]Information obtained from http://en.wikipedia.org/wiki/Gordon_Allport.

[28]Ibid.

[29]G. W. Allport, *The Individual and His Religion* (New York: McMillan, 1950).

[30]Robert Fuller, *Spiritual but Not Religious* (Oxford: Oxford University Press, 2005), 165.

[31]James Fowler, "Stages of Faith," in *Women's Spirituality: Resources for Christian Development,* ed. Joann Wolski Conn (Mahwah, N.J.: Paulist Press, 1986), 226–32.

[32]"Inside Santa Fe's Faith Communities: Journey to Adulthood–Self, Society, Spirituality, and Sexuality," *Santa Fe New Mexican,* June 4, 2005.

[33]Ibid.

[34]Ibid.

[35]Ibid.

[36]Information obtained from http://www.clerministries.org/.

[37]Ibid.

[38]Information obtained from http://www.daveramsey.com/etc/cms/kids_teens_money_5195.htmlc.

Addiction

[1]Romans 7:15, 19, 24.

[2]Information obtained from http://en.wikipedia.org/wiki/Addiction.

[3]All twelve steps are in an online edition of Alcoholics Anonymous's Big Book, http://www.aa.org/bigbookonline/en_BigBook_chapt5.pdf, 59.

[4]Fred Craddock and Eugene Boring, *The People's New Testament Commentary* (Louisville: Westminster John Knox Press, 2004), 486.

[5]Information obtained from "Foreword to Fourth Edition" at http://www.aa.org/bigbookonline/en_f4e.cfm.

[6]Ibid.

[7]Information obtained from "The Twelve Traditions" at http://www.aa.org/bigbookonline/en_f4e.cfm.

[8]Department of Health and Human Services, *Results from the 2005 National Survey on Drug Use and Health: National Findings.* Report obtained from http://www.oas.samhsa.gov/nsduh/2k5nsduh/2k5results.htm#7.1.2.

[9]Ibid.

[10]Information obtained from http://www.addictionintervention.com/intervention/index.asp.

[11]Information obtained from http://www.addictionintervention.com/intervention/what_is_int_fa.asp.

[12]Information obtained from http://www.addictionintervention.com/intervention/10_steps.asp.

[13]"How Young Adults Obtain Prescription Pain Relievers for Nonmedical Use," The NSDUH (National Survey on Drug Use and Health) Report 39, (2006). Report obtained from http://www.oas.samhsa.gov/2k6/getPain/getPain.htm.

[14]"Characteristics of Young Adult (Aged 18-25) and Youth (Aged 12-17) Admissions: 2004," The Dasis (Drug and Alcohol Information System) Report 21 (2006). Report obtained from http://www.oas.samhsa.gov/2k6/youngTX/youngTX.htm.

[15]Bernard P. Horn, "Is There a Cure for America's Gambling Addiction?" Article obtained from http://www.pbs.org/wgbh/pages/frontline/shows/gamble/procon/horn.html.

[16]Information obtained from http://pursuit-of-perfection.com/teenagers_and_eating_disorders.html.

[17]Michele Staton et al., "Risky Sex Behavior and Substance Use among Young Adults," *Health and Social Work* 24, no. 2 (1999).

[18]Richard Reeves, "Does Sex Make Us Happy? Don't Talk about It. Our Satisfaction in Bed Is Not Rising in Relation to the Public Obsession with Open Sexuality–In Fact, Quite the Opposite," *New Statesman,* March 28, 2005.

[19]Ibid.

God of Rock

[1]Information obtained from http://www.surefish.co.uk/culture/features/141004_xian_music_fair_question.htm.

Who May Serve?

[1]Information obtained from http://www.lpts.edu/About_Us/President_Newsletter.asp?id=7.

[2]Ibid.

[3]Information obtained from http://www.acfnewsource.org/religion/starting_over.html.

[4]Kathy Furlong, "Serving a Changing Student Population: The End of the 'Typical' Seminary Student." Article obtained from http://seminarygradschool.com/38320.

[5]Art Jester, "Duke Divinity Professor Bemoans State of Clergy," *Lexington Herald-Leader,* January 20, 2001.

[6]George Neumayr, "Liberal Catholicism's Just Deserts," www.theamericanprowler.org, March 1, 2002.

[7]Information obtained from http://newark.rutgers.edu/~lcrew/koinonia.html.

[8]Ibid.

[9]Sam Hodges, "Baptists at Odds over Removal of Female Professor," *Dallas Morning News,* January 19, 2007.

[10]Information obtained from http://www.usatoday.com/news/religion/2006-06-19-episcopal-reaction_x.htm.

[11]Sally Geis and Donald Messer, eds., *Caught in the Crossfire: Helping Christians Debate Homosexuality* (Nashville: Abingdon Press, 1994).

[12]Ibid., 80–81.

[13]Ibid.

[14]Information obtained from http://www.gaytoz.com/bResearch.asp.

[15]Pew Research Center, *How Young People View Their Lives, Futures and Politics: A portrait of 'Generation Next,'* January 2007, 3.

[16]Ibid., 3.

[17]Marvin Read, "Churchmen of All Stripes to Discuss Gay Issues," *The Pueblo Chieftain,* January 20, 2007.

[18]Ibid.

Church of the Prodigal Child

[1]Robert W. Fairlie, "Are We Really a Nation Online? Ethnic and Racial Disparities in Access to Technology and Their Consequences," Leadership Conference on Civil Rights Education Fund, September 20, 2005, 2.

[2]William Mahedy and Janet Bernardi, *A Generation Alone: Xers Making a Place in the World* (Downers Grove, Ill.: InterVarsity Press, 1994), 56.

[3]Alexandra Robbins and Abby Wilner, *Quarterlife Crisis: The Unique Challenges of Life in Your Twenties* (New York: Tarcher, 2001), 29.

[4]Ibid., 30.

[5]Ibid., 35.

[6]Mahedy and Bernardi, *A Generation Alone,* 17–18.

[7]Ibid., 56.

[8]Robert Fuller, *Spiritual but Not Religious* (Oxford: Oxford University Press, 2005), 13.

[9]Ibid., 15.

[10]Ibid., 18–19.

[11]Ibid.

[12]Ibid., 21.

[13]Ibid., 75–77.